I gladly commend this book to you because it [...]
ant to say to the UK church that we desperatel[...]
alone, this comes from their heart, is biblical a[...]
They are practitioners of what they preach. Be [...]

Roy Godwin, author of *The Grace Outpouring* and *The Way of Blessing*.

Wanting a church for the poor is easy. Knowing how to build one requires wisdom and skill. Martin and Natalie are helpful guides for anyone who wants to move beyond desire and into action.

Phil Moore, leader of Everyday Church, London, author of *Gagging Jesus* and the *Straight to the Heart* Bible commentaries.

Praise God for a book profoundly rooted in biblical principles and filled with shining and authentic practical application. Thoroughly inspirational.

Terry Virgo, founder of Newfrontiers.

Jesus told us that he had been 'anointed by the Holy Spirit to bring good news to the poor'. We constantly need to ask ourselves whether the way we live, speak, and act meets that high threshold; whether we use our gifts, voices, and privileges in the service of the most vulnerable—for whom the news is rarely good and for whom life often goes from bad to worse. This wonderful book points us in the right direction.

Lord David Alton, cross bench peer.

This insightful book serves as a timely wake-up call to church leaders and members everywhere that just as the gospel is good news for the poor, so surely our churches must be the same. With a powerful blend of compassionate concern and careful attention to biblical principles, Martin and Natalie write honestly from both the heart and the head.

Livy Gibbs, conference speaker and part of the leadership team at Emmanuel Church, London.

This book is both inspiring and deeply practical. Pointing out the recent surge 'in church engagement with the poor', and reminding us that revival 'almost always starts with the poor', it observes that our churches remain largely middle class. But there's real encouragement here about the possibility of change, and practical advice about how to bring it about.

Rt. Hon. Stephen Timms MP.

With startling statistics, profound insights, and biblical truth, *A Church for the Poor* educates and illustrates about the reality of poverty in our society. It challenges the church to fulfil its God-given mandate and eradicate poverty in all its expressions.

Pastor Tope Koleoso, Jubilee Church London.

We are very fortunate to have this excellent book to help us integrate people from all walks of society among us as the church. I highly recommend you read it; devour it; put it into practice; and put a copy in as many hands as possible. Let's be good news to the poor, restoring dignity, hope and love in this next season. It is time!

Angela Kemm, international speaker and evangelist.

When it comes to social transformation, nothing carries more potential than the local church. But so often we fall short. This brilliant and ruggedly practical book could make all the difference. Tackling tough questions and offering robust answers, the authors provide us with a wealth of arguments, ideas and examples in favour of a church for the poor. This book isn't simply another 'must-read' Christian text. Reading it won't be enough. This book demands more attention. This is **'must-study'** stuff: leaders and congregations will have to grapple with the issues. That is what it will take to build the church for the poor that society and the future so desperately needs.

Chris Mould, Chief Executive of the Foundation for Social Change and Inclusion; former Chief Executive of the Trussell Trust foodbank network.

A CHURCH FOR THE POOR

Transforming the church to reach
the poor in Britain today

**MARTIN CHARLESWORTH
& NATALIE WILLIAMS**

David C Cook®
transforming lives together

A CHURCH FOR THE POOR Published by David C Cook, 4050 Lee Vance Drive, Colorado Springs, CO 80918 U.S.A.

Integrity Music Limited, a division of David C Cook., Eastbourne, East Sussex BN23 6NT, England

The graphic circle C logo is a registered trademark of David C Cook.

ISBN 978-0-8307-7213-1

The Cook Team: Ian Matthews, Jennie Pollock, Jo Stockdale.

Cover Design: Mark Prentice, beatroot.media

Cover Image: Adobe stock

Typesetting by Zaccmedia

Printed in the United Kingdom

First Edition 2017
1 2 3 4 5 6 7 8 9 10

CONTENTS

FOREWORD

The church that Jesus planted was a church for the poor. He described his vision for the church when he told his disciples in Matthew 26:11 that, 'The poor you will always have with you.' The question is therefore quite sobering: Do we? Do we actually have the poor among us in our churches today?

For many churches, the answer is a definite no. Somewhere along the way, those churches became a respectable haunt for the middle classes instead of a radical haven of hope for the poor, the oppressed and the marginalised. Churches are closing down across the Western world and, by and large, the poor aren't noticing because the poor are not among them. Those churches checked out of Jesus' mission many years before they closed their doors.

Many of us care passionately about this. We long to see the church return to the initial vision that Jesus described to his disciples. We feel as passionate about it as the apostle Paul when he returned excitedly from visiting the other apostles in Jerusalem: 'All they asked was that we should continue to remember the poor, the very thing I had been eager to do all along' (Gal. 2:10). Like Paul, many of us are eager to create churches for the poor—places where the least and the lost and the lonely can find the love of Jesus Christ in the eyes and the arms of his people.

The problem is that most of us don't really know where to begin. We don't know how to turn our deep desire into concrete action on the ground. That's where this book comes in. Martin Charlesworth and Natalie Williams have produced a manual that will help you turn your desire into action. They draw upon their own experience in cutting-edge church ministry to the poor to inspire and equip you to take wise steps forward in your own context today. I have been to both of their churches and seen some of what they write about in action. I commend them to you whole-heartedly as guides for your journey towards turning your own church outwards to embrace the poor.

Martin and Natalie draw on a wealth of personal experience, but they also draw on a deep understanding of the Bible's teaching about helping those trapped by poverty. They recognise the principle of Job 29:16, that eager desire needs to be accompanied by thorough research of the problem. Job was able to tell his friends that 'I investigated the case of the person I did not know.' Martin and Natalie also recognise that helping those in need requires a wise and concrete plan. Their book embodies the principle of Proverbs 13:4, that 'The lazy person eagerly desires yet gets nothing, but the desires of the diligent are fully satisfied.'

So well done for picking up this book. You have already started out on the journey towards transforming your church into *A Church for the Poor*. Read on and let Martin and Natalie guide you forward in your journey. Highlight, underline and scribble notes in the margin—do whatever it takes to turn their wisdom into concrete action on the ground.

One day Jesus will return from heaven to ask his followers whether they built churches for the poor. He prophesies about that day in Matthew 25:34-36, 40

> Come, you who are blessed by my Father; take your inheritance, the kingdom prepared for you since the creation of the world. For I was hungry and you gave me something to eat, I was thirsty and you gave me something to drink, I was a stranger and you invited me in, I needed clothes and you clothed me, I was ill and you looked after me, I was in prison and you came to visit me … Truly I tell you, whatever you did for one of the least of these brothers and sisters of mine, you did for me.

On that day, we will not regret our efforts to respond to the vision Jesus has for his church. May this book help you to rejoice on that day that you worked with him to create *A Church for the Poor*.

Phil Moore
Everyday Church, London, UK
May 2017

ACKNOWLEDGEMENTS

There are many people who have played a part in this book being written and published, often quietly but resolutely supporting the authors behind the scenes. As always, special thanks is due to the other members of the Jubilee+ team—Andy Biggs and Pete and Sue Lyndon—for your prayers and support, to our wonderful administrator Sheena Gardner and to the Jubilee+ directors.

Thank you to Annmarie Moran for assisting with research in the early stages and to Ben Lindsay for invaluable insights. Thank you to Annmarie, Phil Moore, Katherine Blessan, Karen Williams, Geoff Knott and Paul Mann for valuable feedback on the draft text.

We have greatly appreciated the support, prayer and advice of the Jubilee+ consultation group, especially Angela Kemm, Dave Fellingham and Ginny Burgin.

Jeremy Simpkins continues to provide us with steadfast oversight and passion for what we are doing. Thank you.

We are so grateful to the team at David C Cook for your commitment to this book, especially to Ian Matthews for your passion for publishing it and to the gifted and helpful Jennie Pollock for editing that enabled us to say what we really meant.

Martin would also like to thank his wife Jane, his family and the leaders and members of Barnabas Community Church in Shrewsbury for the many ways they have supported him in this project and released him for the work of Jubilee+.

Natalie would also like to thank the amazing friends who have supported her through the process of this book being developed and written: Dorothy Bourdet, Santino and Emma Hamberis, Caner and Joanna Mutu, Sarah Owen, Nic and Hannah Beaney, Richard and Anna Wilson, Paul and Hazel Woods, Paul and Chloe Mann, Claire Lockwood, and too many others to mention. Natalie thanks her wonderful King's Church Hastings family. And as always, she would like to thank her incredible mum.

ABOUT THE AUTHORS

Martin Charlesworth

Martin lives in Shrewsbury with his wife Jane and has three grown-up daughters. He holds degrees in history and theology, and worked as a teacher and in business before becoming a church leader. Martin led Barnabas Community Church Shrewsbury from 1994 to 2014 and helped develop its strong emphasis on social action and community engagement.

In his spare time, Martin enjoys cycling, squash and mountaineering. He is an enthusiastic traveller, having previously lived in Pakistan and South Africa.

Martin leads Jubilee+.

Natalie Williams

Natalie grew up in a working class family in Hastings, one of the most deprived areas of Britain. She was the first person in her family to go to university. After graduating, she worked as a journalist in London and Beijing. She has an MA in Political Communications.

Natalie now works for King's Church Hastings, where she oversees communications and social action, and for Jubilee+ as communications coordinator.

She is passionate about Christians and churches being a force for good in their communities and actively demonstrating the mercy of God to those in need.

ABOUT JUBILEE+

The Jubilee+ vision is to see the church in the UK be a champion of the poor and a means to healthy communities across the nation.

This is a big vision. It's based on the fact that we believe we serve a big God whose heart is especially inclined towards the poor. We also believe that his church has a responsibility not only to care for and empower those in need, but also to speak up on behalf of the voiceless.

Our vision goes beyond seeing individual lives transformed—as important as that is—to seeing entire neighbourhoods and communities strengthened so that our society as a whole is healthier. Our conviction is that when churches are at the heart of social action, social justice and social enterprise, society flourishes.

Jubilee+ was formed in 2011, initially to serve Newfrontiers churches in the UK. Since our inception we have run many national conferences, spoken at numerous events around the country, delivered training to churches across the UK, held roadshows, lobbied politicians and other key decision-makers, published our first book—*The Myth of the Undeserving Poor*—in 2014, conducted some insightful research into the difference churches are making in their localities, gained charitable status, and had regular contact with a wide range of churches of various denominations in the UK.

Today, we equip churches of all denominations to engage more effectively with our communities and particularly to increase their capacity to serve the poor.

We hope we will be an encouragement as we, together, seek to enable the church to be highly effective in its integrated mission to preach Christ and demonstrate his love for our communities.

Find us at: *www.jubilee-plus.org* | *www.facebook.com/jubileeplus* | *www.twitter.com/jubileeplus*

INTRODUCTION

Julie was homeless, in filthy clothes, hungry, and desperate, with nowhere else to turn, when she first came to my (Natalie's) church building looking for help. She didn't have any family locally who could put her up. Her few friends were facing similar crises themselves.

Our first response was to give Julie some food and book her into a bed and breakfast for the night. Next, we directed her to local organisations that could provide support. We made phone calls on her behalf, and provided some financial help and a lot of emotional support. Julie started coming to church and reading the Bible. After some time, she came to believe in Jesus and was baptised. Her material and emotional needs continued, and the church invested lots of time and energy in supporting Julie. We continued to help with food and electricity. A number of people in the church spent many, many hours with her, in friendship and support. Within a couple of months of being baptised, Julie returned to some of her old destructive patterns of behaviour, including unhelpful past relationships. She began to drift from church and from her friendships with other Christians. She comes back every now and then, particularly when she is in need, but she hasn't been meaningfully involved in church life or in relationships with her friends from church for many months now.

Does this example sound familiar to you? For every story we hear of someone making the journey from homelessness to church-based support to becoming a Christian to ending up leading others out of poverty and to Jesus, there seem to be dozens of Julies. We could resent the fact that Julie and hundreds like her keep reappearing when they face a new crisis, or we can be grateful that they know that our churches will welcome them time after time. Either way, we long for the stories of complete redemption, where people turn to churches to find their every need—material, physical, emotional, relational and spiritual— met in Jesus Christ. Yet when we travel to churches across the country speaking on social justice and social action, time and time again we hear stories like Julie's, and we are asked how to build churches where those facing poverty can be fully integrated into church life alongside the middle class and the affluent. It seems to be a common theme, crossing geographical, urban/rural, ethnic and denominational boundaries.

This book addresses a tough but exciting subject. The market is not crowded when it comes to practical books on the church and poverty in the UK. We, the authors, did not rush to write it—we felt compelled. We don't write with all the answers, but we do write from the heart. We're both committed to local churches that are engaging with the poor. What we know we have learnt either on the ground in our churches or from our friends doing similar things all across the UK.

This is a book of two halves. In the first half we start with our very different personal stories, which explain what we have experienced and what motivates us. We then set the scene by exploring the context of poverty in Britain today, including who the poor actually are in our society. A biblical perspective on poverty is obviously fundamentally important to our understanding of how we are to build churches for the poor, and we examine that in chapter three. We follow this with brief reflections on church-based care for the poor in Britain, before looking at some of the obstacles facing our churches today, such as lingering class divisions in our communities.

In the second half of the book we move on to practicalities. Transforming our churches to meaningfully reach the poor in Britain today requires us to think about our calling and our culture, strategy and capacity, keys we need and counting the cost.

We have a big vision to see churches of all denominations, in all areas of the country, becoming diverse families for everyone, regardless of class, wealth, social status or any other potential barrier. We hope this book will play its part in seeing that vision increasingly become a reality.

ONE

WHO ARE WE?

In many respects we are quite unlikely co-authors, perhaps even unlikely to be united in a shared passion and pursuit to see the church in the UK as a champion for the poor in our communities. We are very different people who live in very different places and who come from very different backgrounds. So we thought we'd start by telling you a little about who we are and what drives us.

Martin's story

The more I think of it, the more I can say that I am one of the least likely people to be writing a book like this—or even to be involved in the issues it discusses.

I grew up in a secure middle class English home. My parents saved up to enable me to go to a private boarding school. I did well at school. I was an independent-minded teenager with strong opinions and a keen interest in exploring life and the world. I had little sense of weakness or need. Everything was going well.

Then something surprising happened. I was fifteen when one of my teachers told me that he was a Christian—in a personal and living kind of a way! This really was a surprise. I had not heard of such people before. My limited experience of the church had been formal and dry. In fact, I was drifting away from religion just at that very time and beginning to think about radical political ideas instead.

Anyway, to cut a long story short, my teacher patiently explained about the message of Jesus—his death, resurrection and offer of new spiritual life. Somehow I became intrigued. So I set myself a test. I would study the resurrection of Jesus to see if the evidence stood up to scrutiny. History was my favourite subject at the time and I was interested in evidence. To my surprise and wonder I found that the resurrection was hard to refute. Soon afterwards I became a Christian.

However, the faith I had been born into was focused on personal discipleship rather than church community life. Also, no one mentioned to me at the time anything about social justice or poverty or God's concern for the marginalised. It is not that I didn't theoretically believe those things were important, but they did not impinge on my life.

All this changed through a surprising invitation. While still at school, a friend recommended to me that I have a gap year and go to work for someone he knew in South Africa. That someone was a Dr Guy Daynes, a medical missionary from the UK, who was working in rural South Africa (Transkei). I arrived at the height of apartheid in 1978. Political tension was in the air. Racial injustices were there for all to see. Even on the overnight steam train I took on my arrival in Johannesburg to my destination station of Pieter-maritzburg, I was forced to face the reality of a bitterly divided society: segregated rail carriages, racist sentiments from the soldier with whom I shared a sleeping compartment, homeless families sleeping rough near the railway stations.

Dr Daynes was committed to the health of some of the poorest citizens in South Africa—the rural poor. I worked alongside him and his patients in a remote rural hospital. I also travelled widely. I saw the poverty of the black townships, the social segregation of the cities, and the great wealth of so many white people. This all provoked so many questions and emotions. Perhaps the most distressing day I spent there was visiting the well-known Soweto township, on the edge of Johannesburg. Two years earlier Soweto had erupted into rioting and many had been killed or injured as the police suppressed the riot. It made headlines around the world. I had seen it on my TV screen in the UK—now I was there in person. Travelling through the township is an experience I shall never forget. There was so much poverty so close to the affluence of the white suburbs of nearby Johannesburg. Wealth and poverty can co-exist in such close proximity—anywhere in the world. We have to link those two worlds together.

What changed me the most was to see active racially integrated churches engaged with social justice and caring for the poor. Suddenly it became clear to me that the coming of God's kingdom involved dealing directly with urgent human needs and social issues—as an outworking of our personal salvation and as a key part of discipleship.

By the time I came back to the UK I was a different person with a different outlook. I determined to live my Christian life always in the light of the urgent needs of the poor and marginalised. I have found many ways to do this over the years that have passed since then. It is that journey that led me to where I am now—writing this book.

Natalie's story

My background is very different to Martin's, yet I've still taken a somewhat circular route to discovering God's heart for the poor.

I grew up in a very working class family. By the government's definition of relative poverty as a household where the income is below 60 percent of the national median, we were poor. I didn't really know it at the time, though there were signs of it. I had free school meals for a few years at primary school, we didn't go on holidays abroad but to Pontin's every other year, my dad went from job to job (frozen food store manager to double-glazing salesman to taxi driver) before a back injury put him out of work and onto benefits. I wanted violin lessons when I was a young child but was told we couldn't afford it. And I remember my parents agreeing to let me go on a secondary school trip to Spain but finding half-way through the instalments that they were unable to pay, so my grandparents stepped in to cover the costs.

However, it wasn't until I went to university (the first person in my extended family to do so) that I realised my experience wasn't the same as everyone else's. When fellow students were shocked that I hadn't owned a passport or been on a plane until a few days before my twenty-second birthday, I was surprised. I hadn't even thought about it, let alone considered that it was unusual compared to my peers.

There were other ways in which I did know my experiences were different. I was sixteen when my parents split up, and I could count my friends from single parent families on one hand, even though I went to the poorest performing secondary school in a seaside town well known for its levels of deprivation.

When I became a Christian, at fifteen, I started to be more aware of my background, but mostly in terms of seeing how my life had in all likelihood been diverted down a different path. For example, many of the girls in my tutor group had their first child before they hit twenty. I'm sure I would have done likewise.

However, I also noticed social settings in which I felt uncomfortable—being invited to someone's house for dinner was a new experience, with multiple opportunities for anxiety. For example, when food was put onto the table in different serving bowls and I was told to help myself first, as the guest, I didn't really know what to do and wished the hosts would go first so I could copy them.

There were many similar situations, some I've only reflected on with hindsight. I know that God has used them to shape my current views on class and poverty, but I cannot in all honesty say that they made me particularly compassionate or kind-hearted towards people in need.

As I became an adult, I became more aware of how I was shaped by certain experiences. For example, when I got myself into huge amounts of debt and didn't know where to turn; when I lived and worked as a journalist in Beijing for a year; or when I worked in my hometown for a local partnership of the police, council, fire service and others. The latter, in particular, was where I started to feel a deepening concern about people trapped in poverty, especially where there was a lack of hope for real transformation. It was in that role that I started to feel increasingly disturbed about injustice and about how media and political narratives can so easily shape our views. I saw that they can subtly and overtly mould our pre-conceptions (at best) and prejudices (at worst). And it was in that job that I started to notice that no one, at the time, seemed to be asking what the church had to say about deep-rooted, long-established problems in local communities.

All of these experiences have influenced me, but over the last few years I have made a concentrated effort to study the Bible to see if there is a Christian perspective on poverty, even when the causes of it are far from simple. As a result, a journey has started in my heart (and will no doubt continue for a long time) towards increased mercy, generosity, compassion, kindness and love. My attitudes have changed. Aspects of my lifestyle have changed. I'm a work in progress, but at this point in time I'm more passionate than I've ever been that the church not only has a vital role to play in alleviating poverty and supporting people out of poverty, but that it actually has *the* vital role in these things. It is the hope of the world; the only 'organisation' that offers real, absolute and lasting change. So it must do and be all that it is supposed to do and be. We hope this book can help many churches on that journey.

PART ONE
A church for the poor—setting the scene

TWO

WHO ARE THE POOR? AND WHY SHOULD WE CARE?

Poverty—the debate

A generation of UK children will suffer in poverty. Suddenly that's normal.

The Guardian, November 2016

Scandal of Benefits Britain: 6-bed mansion for sponger family of 12 ... and YOU pay!

Daily Star, October 2013

Britain's divided decade: the rich are 64% richer than before the recession, while the poor are 57% poorer.

The Independent, March 2015

Half of households receive more in benefits than they pay in taxes.

The Telegraph, June 2015

Child poverty in Britain is causing 'social apartheid'.

The Observer, August 2013

Revealed: The real number of Britons mired in poverty is HALF the official total ...

Daily Mail, May 2015

It's not difficult to find excuses to avoid helping the poor in Britain today, even for Christians. Spend time chatting to people in your street or your church about poverty, and it won't be long before someone pipes up that there's no real poverty here, or that we should only help those who didn't get themselves into the mess they're in now.

Poverty in Britain is a hotly debated subject. There is no shortage of opinion or emotion. The media regularly weigh into the discussion with sensational stories. Stigmatisation of the poor is on the rise.[1] The political parties are deeply divided in their analysis of both the problem and the possible solutions. Then, to complicate matters further, the devolved governments of the country have rarely seen eye-to-eye with Westminster on social policy and welfare issues. Alongside this, the charity sector has frequently and firmly raised its voice of concern or protest over key political policies.

Then there are the churches. This is the surprising and unexpected story of the early twenty-first century. Just when secularists and cynics were expecting the apparently declining church to sail off into the sunset, it has done the exact opposite! Churches have mobilised themselves in an extraordinary way in recent years to address issues of poverty and need across the country. The foodbank movement has been at the forefront of this activism as it has spread with great speed across the UK in the years following the financial crisis of 2008-09. So pervasive have been church-based foodbanks that commentators and politicians have coined the phrase 'Foodbank Britain' to describe the present state of need and deprivation across the UK. Domestic poverty is now a central political issue. In the 2015 general election campaign, BBC commentator Jeremy Paxman sensationally asked the Prime Minister, David Cameron, as his opening question in a pre-election interview: 'Prime Minister, how many foodbanks are there in Britain?' Such a question would have been inconceivable even five years earlier when foodbanks were hardly known. Domestic poverty is now a hot issue firmly at the centre of public debate.

However, if we cast our minds back just a few years we quickly realise this hasn't always been the case. At the turn of the twenty-first century our country was awash with millennial optimism. All the talk was of ambitious schemes to tackle the huge problems of poverty in the wider world—especially the developing nations. Those were the days of the 'Millennium Development goals'.[2] They were the days when popular campaigns focused on cancelling the unpayable debts of poorer nations, tackling environmental degradation worldwide, maximising international aid and curtailing the power of multi-national companies to exploit poorer nations. Poverty issues back home in the UK seemed relatively small and did not capture the public imagination at the time. Political leaders then were optimistic about making inroads into domestic poverty through robust government interventions.

The national mood has changed significantly since those years around the turn of the century. The main focus has moved decisively and suddenly from the developing world to our own backyard here in Britain. Why has there been such a big change in such a short time?

It all goes back to the dramatic events of those dark days in the summer and autumn of 2008 when the Western world experienced a sudden and critical economic shock—'the credit crunch'. Those who watched news bulletins at that time will recall the extraordinary announcements of well-known banks closing, of eye-wateringly large government bailouts, of anxious building society investors queuing in the streets waiting to withdraw their money, of crisis meetings of central bankers, and of statements of reassurance from nervous politicians. The overheating of the banking system and the over-extension of credit facilities nearly brought the whole economic system crashing down as banks were unable to meet their obligations and literally ran out of cash reserves. The system survived—but only just. Last minute political actions across the Western world just about held the system together—but at great long-term cost.

Soon 'the credit crunch' turned into 'the financial crisis'. Then recession followed. This was an economic turning point in the UK. Government debts soared spectacularly, heavy job losses spread, the housing market came under extreme pressure, businesses were starved of loan capital, government budgets began to be drastically cut. It was a huge change with significant impacts on all parts of UK society. The financial crisis of 2008-09 was not a brief economic blip. Rather, it was a systemic failure with serious long-term consequences. The biggest issue overall has been the severely reduced financial capacity of central governments due to unprecedented levels of peacetime sovereign debt. This indebtedness will take decades to deal with. Thus, we entered suddenly into a new economic era. Few saw it coming, but we all have to live with the consequences.

The consequences of the fallout from the financial crash have been felt much more severely at the bottom end of the economic scale in Britain. This is easily forgotten by the relatively economically secure and affluent majority of Britons. There has been a significant 'squeeze' on people in the middle, leading Prime Minister Theresa May to identify this group as 'just about managing' (or 'JAMs') in 2016. However, the big issue for us as we consider poverty is that the economic turbulence arising from the financial crisis of 2008-09 led to major and seemingly permanent changes in social policy that have seriously impacted the weakest and poorest in Britain. We were suddenly catapulted into an 'age of austerity'.

What were the main changes? Firstly, huge budget cuts for local government funding, leading in time to drastic cuts in public services. Secondly, major welfare reforms with resultant benefits cuts for many and the significant increase in sanctioning recipients of benefits. Areas such as national security and education have been prioritised over welfare. Thirdly, a rethinking of whose responsibility it is to help people out of poverty—government, local community, charities, or individuals themselves? This rethink has tended to place more responsibility on the individual and less on the state. Alongside this there has been an increasing reliance on the charitable sector to fill the gaps being left by reducing state provision. Finally, there has been an increasing tendency to attribute responsibility for poverty itself to the poor, who, to some extent, have again become 'the undeserving poor'.

This is the process that has generated such heated debate about poverty here in the UK. We could devote considerable space here to following the nuances and contours of the debate. However, since our main focus is on the practical role of the church, we leave that complex story for others to tell more fully.

So what has been the response of the church to these new, challenging circumstances? Across all denominations there has been a mass mobilisation of churches to address some of the immediate and long-term needs that have come to the fore. We discussed this process in more detail in our last book, *The Myth of the Undeserving Poor*.[3] There we described the dramatic emergence and development of what we might call the 'community franchise' methodology that has enabled churches to start literally hundreds of locally-based social action projects covering a wide range of needs.[4] In this model an effective social action project is replicated quickly by creating a franchise system in which the originator trains and equips church-based local groups to run similar projects that are managed locally but resourced from a national network. However, even within this surge of activism, deeper strategic questions have emerged. Response to immediate need is one thing, but it can't be sustained and built upon without careful reflection about underlying issues raised by the context. It is to some of these issues that we will now turn. These are issues that are commonly discussed in churches as individual Christians and church communities grapple with understanding both the context they are working in and the rationale for what they are doing.

Why should we bother addressing poverty in the UK when poverty is so much greater in the developing world?

There is an important distinction in the poverty debate—the difference between 'absolute' and 'relative' poverty. Virtually all commentators accept this distinction. Absolute poverty means the lack of the most essential basic needs for pure survival, such as shelter, clothing, food and clean water. This is a lack that fundamentally threatens health, wellbeing and even life itself. African farmers whose crops have comprehensively failed are absolutely poor, homeless refugees are absolutely poor, victims of modern slavery are absolutely poor, direct victims of severe flooding whose houses have been washed away are absolutely poor. No one disputes this. It is obvious. Let us not mistake the point: the needs of the absolutely poor throughout the world must be a top priority for the church. Nothing should diminish the mandate for Christians to play their part in the relief of absolute poverty wherever they can. However, it is a false dichotomy to set absolute poverty elsewhere against less extreme ('relative') poverty at home in the UK. This is not an either-or situation. Relative poverty has serious impacts on hundreds of thousands of Britons. It may be less likely to kill them, but it can destroy or damage their lives, as we will discuss shortly. We cannot ignore our neighbours in our communities simply because of the needs of those in developing nations. We must support international charities, political initiatives and specific church-based projects at the same time as helping those who struggle to feed their families or heat their homes in the street next door. We cannot use our donations to overseas projects as an excuse to walk by on the other side of the road and ignore the rough sleeper on our high street. Jesus doesn't leave that option open to us: in telling the parable of the Good Samaritan, he makes it abundantly plain that we're to help the person in front of us.

So let's be clear—there can be no ultimate contradiction between the needs of those in absolute and relative poverty. Indeed, to set one against the other may turn out to be an excuse for not facing legitimate needs on our doorsteps.

What exactly is relative poverty?

There may be very little absolute poverty in Britain today—but there is relative poverty, and plenty of it. What do we mean by relative poverty? Much study has been done on this subject in the UK and a carefully considered approach has been developed and used as the basis for extensive research and evaluation.[5] This approach focuses on measures of deprivation rather than on levels of income. Agreeing an appropriate measure of income in this context has been problematic. Also, we all know that other factors have a major influence on actual standards of living such as assets, the number of people to support in each household, the variable cost of living across the country, etc. So, in our view, levels of deprivation are much more effective at measuring poverty.[6]

With this in mind we can define relative poverty as the inability to access basic necessities to live viably in the UK or to play a normal part in our society. Although there will be varied opinions about what constitutes 'basic necessities' (for example, is a tooth-brush a 'basic necessity'? Is internet access?), we should not let this fact take away from the pursuit of a well-researched framework for evaluating the necessities of life in our society.

As it happens, a robust methodology has been developed over recent years. This is based on the use of public opinion rather than more abstract academic measures as the touchstone for a definition. The advantage of this methodology is that it anchors our definitions of deprivation in the norms of our own society.

In 2012, landmark research was conducted, sponsored by the Economic & Social Research Council, with the results published the next year in the *Poverty and Social Exclusion* report.[7] This was the most comprehensive survey of poverty and social exclusion ever undertaken in the UK and followed three earlier studies in 1983, 1990 and 1999.[8] Through interviews with a representative sample of the British public, the researchers were able to draft the following list of items that are considered necessities as the basis for the assessment:

- heating to keep home adequately warm;
- damp-free home;
- two meals a day;
- ability to visit friends or family in hospital or other institutions;
- ability to replace or repair broken electrical goods;
- fresh fruit and vegetables every day;
- celebrations on special occasions;
- all recommended dental treatment;
- warm, waterproof coat;
- ability to attend weddings, funerals and the like;
- meat, fish or vegetarian equivalent every other day;
- curtains or window blinds;
- household contents insurance;
- enough money to keep your home in a decent state of decoration;
- hobby/leisure activity;
- appropriate clothes for job interviews;
- table and chairs at which all the family can eat;
- taking part in sport/exercise activities or classes;
- two pairs of all-weather shoes;

- regular savings of at least £20 per month for future financial challenges;
- regular payments to a pension.[9]

Those who did not have access to three or more items on the list were considered to some extent 'deprived'. As you reflect on this, pause for a minute and ask yourself: what would I feel if several of these basic necessities were unavailable to me through financial hardship? How would this affect my life and that of my family? These are sobering questions. For most people in a secure economic situation the thought of being temporarily deprived of one or two of these necessities can provoke agitation and concern. If that is true for the relatively affluent, how much more for those in poverty who face such deprivations regularly? Comparisons between richer and poorer sections within society are a vital part of addressing poverty meaningfully. This is what we must do in order to get a comprehensive understanding of the issues we face here in the UK.

The research found that about a third of households in the UK today face significant difficulties, specifically:

- Around 4 million people are not properly fed by today's standards.
- Around 2.5 million children live in homes that are damp.
- Around 2.3 million households cannot afford to heat the living areas of their homes.
- Over 30 million people suffer from financial insecurity.[10]

By comparing data with the earlier reports the 2012 survey also found worrying trends concerning the increase in poverty in recent decades. Key findings included:

- The proportion of households falling below society's minimum standards has doubled since 1983.
- More children lead impoverished and restricted lives today than in 1999.
- Five million more people live in inadequate housing than in the 1990s.
- Nine percent of households can't heat their homes adequately today—up from 5 percent in 1983 and 3 percent in 1999.[11]

Does relative poverty in the UK really matter?

Poverty in the UK should matter to Christians for at least three important reasons.

Firstly, it is a serious situation if hundreds of thousands of people in a country as rich as ours cannot afford sufficient nutritious food, cannot afford to adequately heat their homes, experience serious financial insecurity or are overloaded with unpayable debt. It is a serious matter if people are excluded from society because they can't afford to take part in simple leisure or social events. Such problems divide society and demoralise the poorest. No concerned Christian can turn a blind eye to such burning issues. Such concern should not be dimmed by the awareness that some people experience deprivation due in part to their own mistaken actions. We will explore this issue later.

Secondly, the best available research suggests that poverty is on the increase and that the gap between rich and poor is widening.[12] This trend appears to have been ongoing since at least the 1980s and shows no sign of slowing down. It is a matter of social justice to stand up for the poor at a time when the rich are getting steadily richer. Studies have also shown that a widening gap between rich and poor is bad for the whole of society—not just the poor.[13]

Thirdly, it is a serious matter that the rise of poverty has gone hand-in-hand with a hardening of attitudes towards the poor. We have seen in recent times the resurgence of the time-worn tendency to stigmatise the poor and blame them for their plight. This has been especially prominent in the media. We wrote extensively about this phenomenon in our first book, *The Myth of the Undeserving Poor*, to which we refer readers for a more detailed consideration of this issue.[14] However, Christians must not acquiesce to such socially divisive and negative stereotyping. This is especially true when we consider that it is hard to substantiate any distinction between 'strivers' and 'skivers' or the 'deserving' and 'undeserving' among the poor.

Isn't supporting church-based social action enough of a response?

The dramatic increase in church-based social action is an exciting development. Research by Jubilee+ has shown the sheer scale of this growth.[15] The proliferation of church-based foodbanks, debt advice services, job clubs, educational projects, supported housing schemes, elderly support projects and much more are testimony to the energy and vision of churches in the face of increasing social needs of all types. However, the poor and deprived are still sometimes helped at a relational 'arm's length'. The church has more to offer those in need than just social action projects. People are more than 'clients'—outcomes are more than statistics. People need friendship and community. People need to be valued. Many need someone to walk alongside them as they try to find ways of rebuilding their lives. Some can be given jobs in social enterprises and other businesses run by Christians. The full scope of the gospel message is there to be shared. We need to find ways of integrating those from poor or deprived backgrounds into church communities, especially as some embark on a spiritual journey towards faith in Christ. This will be the subject of further consideration in part two of this book.

Does poverty have any other significant dimensions?

Poverty is primarily an economic phenomenon. It is about resources. The central question is: do people have the economic resources they need to live viably in our society? We have to address this question first. However, it is widely recognised that there can be a number of negative aspects of poverty that are not strictly economic but are very significant and damaging. We have identified three such outcomes in our previous book[16] and we will refer back to them briefly now to provide a broader context within which to consider poverty in modern Britain.

Aspirational poverty—the loss of hope

First, let's consider what we call 'aspirational poverty'. Aspiration lifts people up. We dream of making progress in our lives and we then use our skills or energy to seek to fulfil some of those aspirations. Some aspire to education, some to vocational qualifications, some to home ownership, some to a stable family life, some to

parenthood, some to going up the ladder in their workplace ...
Aspiration is about believing that positive change is not only
desirable but also possible for us. Not all aspirations are realistic or
good for us, but to aspire is a normal part of life. To lose hope for
change is a tragic loss to our lives.

However, for many caught in long-term unemployment or
trapped in deprivation, aspiration has been crushed. Hopelessness has
crept in, often followed by depression, cynicism, social isolation and
passivity. We should also remember that, often hidden from view,
children caught in the poverty trap are prone to grow up without
any serious positive aspirations. This in itself is a huge problem.
Those involved in church-based social action will frequently see this
at work among the people they are helping.

Having just written the last paragraph while sitting in a coffee
shop in my (Martin's) home town I walked along the nearby streets
and noticed an old friend sitting begging. John suffers from some
minor special needs, has been unemployed all his adult life and
begs on the streets to supplement his benefits. He has been to our
church foodbank on many occasions and been connected to our
church community. We got talking and he expressed the view that
there was no point trying to get a job. He had been rejected too
many times. He saw himself as unemployable—condemned to a
life on the margins of society. This is aspirational poverty.

The aspiration deficit is one of the burning issues confronting
churches as we engage ever more deeply with poverty. Intuitively
we know that something radical needs to be done. It turns out that
many deprived people need more than crisis intervention or a
shoulder to cry on or a listening ear. They need their confidence

rebuilt in order to face the challenges of their lives. Walking alongside the poor as we seek to help rebuild aspiration turns out to be one of the most creative things Christians can do in becoming a church for the poor. Churches need to tackle aspirational poverty with energy and creativity.

Relational poverty—the loss of community

Then there is 'relational poverty'. We are social creatures. We function best when in community. We need people around us. We need friends. We usually do our best work when working with others. Anyone can get isolated. Even the super-rich can be lonely in their gated homes. However, the poor are at greatest risk of social isolation and what we may call 'relational poverty'. Many have experienced family breakdown, many don't have the confidence to make new friendships, many are scarred by the experience of poverty, many feel they have failed, many suffer mental health problems.

Widespread social mobility now means that extended families are more and more frequently spread far and wide across the country—and even abroad. This puts immediate pressure on those in need. It is harder to call on family members for support if they live many miles away. For those battling with poverty this is a particularly acute problem. Everything from emotional support to childcare to housing often turns out to be hard to get in our modern far-flung family networks.

However, sometimes the church turns out to be the community that gives those with relational needs the best support. Let me tell you about my friend Ray. Ray is long-term unemployed and lives alone in a one-bedroomed council flat. He got connected to our church through a member who was working for a social housing project. Through this friendship, Ray was introduced to our foodbank as a client. Then he became a volunteer and has served faithfully every week for a long time. I have seen Ray twice during the week in which I first drafted this chapter. I saw him at the foodbank team Christmas lunch, quietly enjoying the buzz and the conversation. Then I saw him at the church Christmas carol service—the first time he has been to a church service since we got to know him. Ray has made some new friends and he has found something to live for. He has taken a vital first step out of relational poverty.

Spiritual poverty—the loss of ultimate meaning

Spiritual poverty has reached epidemic proportions in the UK. The cold wind of secularism has blown through our lives sweeping away the remnants of our Christian heritage bit by bit. Formal religion has been on the decline for decades. Even our inherited Christian moral framework is being steadily eroded.

However, spiritual poverty is a particularly acute problem for the poor. With so little else to fall back upon, a lack of spiritual values can lead to an even starker and bleaker life. Those with little to gain from our materialistic society need something deeper to fall back upon in hard times.

The church has an urgent mission to retell the Christian message to the poor. Their spiritual issues must not be neglected in our concern to address their material needs. There can never be a divide between the two. In fact, many people want to discuss spiritual issues in times of need or crisis. The church has made the mistake in the past of dividing social activism from personal evangelism. This is the most unloving thing we can do. God cares for the poor in their current need, but he also cares for their future—their eternal future.

Some time ago Ken and Barbara arrived at the door of the money advice centre at my church. Ken was a supply teacher in his fifties who had got into debt due to lack of work combined with unforeseen repairs needed on his house. Shortly after receiving useful help from the money advice team, Barbara suddenly became seriously ill and died unexpectedly. Ken came back to the money advice team, whom he now saw as friends. They were able to encourage and support him as well as discussing reorganisation of his budget to cope with his new situation. Then Ken was invited to attend Sunday meetings at the church. He found this an eye-opening experience. He had never realised that faith led to such vibrant community life. Shortly afterwards Ken was invited to an Alpha course run by the church. On hearing the gospel message carefully explained, Ken became a Christian and was subsequently baptised and became a member of the church. Ken's problems were not just economic—they were spiritual as well. He found himself on a quest to discover ultimate meaning in life after the tragic events that he had been through. Spiritual poverty often accompanies economic poverty and other stresses—it needs addressing when people are open and seeking answers. A church for the poor will not draw a false distinction between social action and evangelism, and it will not just provide practical assistance. It will boldly and humbly offer the gospel message to answer the deep spiritual poverty that so often exists side-by-side to material poverty.

To be a church for the poor we have to start by facing the real and urgent need of the poor in our nation and in our own communities. We can't filter them out as we live our Christian lives and enjoy our comfortable churches. Once we face it, we need to act: we need to get involved in helping the poor—especially through the projects and ministries of our own churches. Then we need to be willing, where necessary, to stand up with the poor. We also need to respond to the wider problems facing many of those in need—aspirational, relational and spiritual problems. Then, finally, we need to provide a secure and welcoming place for the poor within our church communities where they can respond to the call of Christ and take their full place in church life.

THREE

POVERTY AND THE NEW TESTAMENT CHURCH

As we continue setting the scene for our discussion we are going to visit the New Testament to gain some inspiration for our journey. We are going right back to the very earliest days of the church to try to catch a glimpse of how those early Christians addressed the issue of poverty.

It all started with a sensational event in Jerusalem—the birth of the first church. The coming of the Spirit on the day of Pentecost and the powerful preaching of the apostles had a huge impact. Thousands of residents and visitors to the city came to faith very quickly. The story is well known from the narrative of Acts 2-7. There are lots of interesting things we can say about that vibrant and fast-growing church community. However, there is one side to the story that is often neglected—the fact that there were hundreds of newly baptised church members who were poor and in real need. There were at least three unrelated reasons for this. First, some of the new converts were only visiting Jerusalem for the Pentecost feast when they were converted. They didn't live there. It is reasonable to assume that many stayed on for a time—but without homes or jobs. Second, some of the converts were simply poor in the first place, such as the crippled man who was a beggar on the streets before being healed and converted (Acts 3). It is easy to forget that this new convert did not have any means of support at the time he joined the church. Third, when persecution came it would have had economic consequences: loss of work, theft of property, rejection by family members, and even the need to move out of the city altogether. Persecution has economic consequences. It usually makes its victims poor.

So, what did the church do about the problem of poverty in its midst? Two things: something spontaneous and something organised. First, the spontaneous actions: without any prompting, many church members, seeing the need, shared their possessions around and made direct donations to church funds so that the apostles and other leaders could distribute money as needed. Second, the organised actions: the apostles and other leaders saw the need to set up a food distribution service, especially for some of the widows whose needs were being overlooked. A special team of men was appointed to look after the food distribution (Acts 6:1-6). There is an interesting twist to this story that is easy to miss. The people being overlooked were the widows of the 'Hellenistic' Jews (Acts 6:1). The complaint was that they were being discrimi-nated against because they were 'Hellenistic' Jews rather than 'Hebraic' Jews. What was all that about? Actually, it is interesting and significant to work it out. The Hellenistic Jews were those who mostly lived outside Israel in the Greco-Roman world to the west. The Hebraic Jews were those who lived in Israel or to the east in places such as Parthia. Generally, the Hellenistic Jews were considered less authentic to their Jewish culture—and so were sometimes discriminated against. So here is a case of poverty rooted in personal circumstances (being widows) yet made worse by social stigma. That's something worth remembering. It probably rings a few bells. We'll come back to this issue later on.

To summarise, it seems that the apostles were making a big effort in the Jerusalem church to create a community that accepted all comers, was rooted in personal generosity, was socially inclusive, and had systems in place to help the poorest and most in need.

The next detailed look at a local church we get in the book of Acts is at Antioch (Acts 11:19-30, 13:1-3). The early disciples who had been forced to flee Jerusalem due to persecution (Acts 8:1) started churches in Samaria (Acts 8:4-8) but soon travelled as far north as the large regional capital of Antioch. The church there grew quickly and dynamically under the leadership of Barnabas, Paul and others. It was the first truly multicultural church (Acts 11:19-21 and 13:1). Interestingly, we read that as a result of the words of a visiting prophet, Agabus, they raised money to give to the churches in and around Jerusalem in anticipation of their needs during a predicted food shortage (Acts 11:27-30). This adds another dimension to our understanding of the early church. The people in the Antioch church didn't only consider their own needs—they were also willing to contribute to the economic needs of fellow Christians in far away churches who might fall on hard times. In this way, the more prosperous Antioch Christians identified the equal value and honour of the poorer Judean Christians by giving financially to them, and doing so out of a relational link in Paul and Barnabas who took the gift over to Judea.

Let's fast forward again. Just as the Antioch church was relationally linked to the original Jerusalem church, so the Galatian churches planted by Paul and Barnabas were relationally linked to Antioch. In fact, the Antioch church specifically commissioned Paul and Barnabas to leave them for a time and go to the area we now know as Turkey to preach the gospel and plant churches (Acts 13:1-3). We don't hear too much about the details of everyday life in those new churches in Acts, but we do get a fascinating perspective from reading Paul's letter to the Galatian churches. This was a circular letter written slightly later and designed to be read aloud in these newly planted churches. It contains a vital insight for us.

The key passage for our purposes is Galatians 2:1-10. Here Paul describes a visit he made to Jerusalem to meet some of the original apostles led by Peter. This visit was undertaken in order to confirm the relationship between himself and his co-workers in their mission to the Gentiles on the one hand—and Peter and his fellow apostles in their mission to the Jews on the other. At the time, there had been accusations made by malicious third parties that Paul was an imposter and was preaching a false gospel. Paul was keen to refute this allegation and get the endorsement of Peter. As he recounts the meeting, Paul records that both parties affirmed one another in their respective callings. However, Paul notes one intriguing statement made by the Jerusalem apostles to him at that time: 'All they asked was that we should continue to remember the poor, the very thing I had been eager to do all along' (Gal. 2:10).

What did this mean? And why was it stated? The answers to these questions are vital for our purposes.

Winding the clock back a bit we need to remember that Peter and the Jerusalem-based apostles had responsibility for all the churches they had established in the Judea area—churches that were essentially Jewish. It seems clear that among those Jewish converts they had made a priority of caring for their poorer members and others in need in their localities. There is one fascinating example of this noted in Acts that is incidental to the story—but very significant for our enquiry. Here's how the story is told: As Peter was travelling around Judea he came to a place called Joppa where a church had been established. Unfortunately, at the time he arrived, a much-loved church member had just died. Her name was Dorcas. Peter went to pray for her and miraculously she returned to life. However, what is interesting is the statement made about this godly lady: 'she was always doing good and helping the poor' (Acts 9:36). What a statement! The church members were even able to show Peter some examples of clothes she had made to give away. This seemingly unimportant detail about an ordinary disciple beautifully illustrates the honour given by the early disciples in Judea to those who cared for the poor. This sense of priority came easily to God-fearing Jews such as the apostles due to their knowledge and understanding of the Hebrew Scriptures (the Old Testament) with their emphasis on caring for the poor. This priority had also been hugely underlined by the teaching and example of Jesus himself. So, for Peter, preaching the gospel of Jesus and actively caring for the poor were intrinsically linked. He could not imagine doing one without doing the other. His concern was that

Paul, when working among the Gentiles, might focus exclusively on preaching the gospel and possibly neglect caring for the poor, thus not making it a top priority of church life. Peter feared, no doubt, that a difference may arise between the primarily Jewish churches and the primarily Gentile churches. That is why he and others urged Paul to be intentional and to always 'remember the poor'.

As it turned out, Paul had no difficulty with Peter's challenge. He knew he was called to the Gentiles. He knew he had to work in cultures very different from the Jewish background he came from. But he also knew that the gospel was for people in all cultures and that churches needed to have the same core values within them whatever the race or culture of the members. This is one reason why he knew that the old Jewish religious law (law of Moses) had to go. Its time was up. It was no use in the multicultural world he was now moving in. Paul preached the same message about Jesus Christ wherever he went (1 Cor. 1:22-25), he invoked the power of the same Holy Spirit as the dynamic of church life wherever he went, he built inclusive loving communities wherever he went and—yes, you guessed it—Paul made 'remembering the poor', both within and outside the church, a top priority for any and every church he planted. This was an indispensable sign of an authentic church in the New Testament era.

If that's not convincing enough, let's look at things from a different perspective. As far as we know, the author of the book of James was the James who was the half-brother of Jesus. This James became a well-respected leader in the church at Jerusalem. When he came to write his letter to 'the twelve tribes scattered among the nations' (James 1:1b), he appears to be writing to groups of Jewish disciples who had been forced to relocate from Judea as a result of persecution. James was writing to encourage them to be true to the faith and he brings a wide range of encouragements and challenges to them. No doubt his letter was intended to be read in church gatherings in the different places to which these disciples had been scattered. What is particularly striking about the book is the frequent reference that James makes to issues of social justice, poverty and the like. Here are some key examples that give us a flavour of James' practical and radical approach to this issue:

- The status of individuals does not depend on their wealth, because wealth fades away but God's approval lasts forever (James 1:9-11);
- True faith leads naturally to such things as looking after widows and orphans—and this is something God endorses (James 1:27);
- Churches should never favour the rich in their community life (James 2:1-7);
- God bestows special blessing on those who are poor by the world's standards (James 2:5);
- The church needs to speak out against wealthy people who exploit their workers (James 5:1-6);
- It is not okay for people to live 'in luxury and self-indulgence' while there are people in need around us (James 5:5).

When you think about it, this is quite a formidable list of statements and commands! James did not pull his punches. He was quite clear: the church needs to be a community that really cares for those in need, that does not give undue precedence to the richer members, and that speaks out fearlessly when it sees economic exploitation taking place. This all makes sense when we think back to that vital conversation between Paul, Peter and others in which it was agreed that in all the churches there was an apostolic priority to 'remember the poor'.

We could go on. We could look at other texts. We could discuss Paul's encouragement of the slave-owner Philemon to let his slave Onesimus get his freedom (Philem. 15-16). We could mention the large collection Paul took up in some of his churches to help the impoverished churches of Judea (2 Cor. 8-9). We could discuss the breaking down of social barriers between slave and free in the churches (Gal. 3:28). We could mention the list of needy widows that the church in Ephesus supported (1 Tim. 5:1-16).

But it's not necessary to say any more. The pattern is the same wherever we look: all New Testament churches focused on remembering the poor in whatever way was most relevant to them. It was a priority, not an option.

We need to find relevant ways to follow their example if our churches are to be New Testament churches in any meaningful sense.

FOUR

THE CHURCH, THE NATION AND THE POOR—AN HISTORICAL PERSPECTIVE

History is a great teacher—and never more so than with the history of the church. Now that we have looked at an overview of the New Testament church, our enquiry naturally leads us to reflect on what has happened in Britain in previous generations over this vital question of a church for the poor.

Come with me (Martin) in your historical imagination to the early eighteenth century—three hundred years ago. What was the church like in those days? I'm afraid that the story is rather grim. The institution of the Church of England dominated the nation as the established church, but it did not engage the loyalty and affection of most citizens. It supported the political establishment and the status-quo. Those were days of nominal religious faith, a generally corrupt clergy and a widespread scepticism about the full claims of the Christian message. Most people believed in God in a conceptual sense, but few had a significant personal faith. It was necessary to be in church on Sundays to be seen and to be respectable, but nothing more than that. This was an age in which church was linked to class. In parish churches up and down the country, the wealthy and important sat at the front in reserved seats while the common people sat at the back. Meanwhile, Nonconformity (churches outside the Church of England) was small and marginal to national life due to legal restrictions on non-Anglicans in public life. Being a Nonconformist made you unpopular in many circles. Small groups of sincere believers gathered together in the chapels of the Baptists, Quakers and others. Likewise, the Catholic Church was tolerated, but only with suspicion, as Catholics had often been linked to subversive political activities in the previous two centuries.

Into this stagnant situation burst the Methodist movement in the 1740s. It was an astonishing contrast to the rest of the church. John Wesley and George Whitefield spearheaded an audacious attempt to preach an evangelical gospel to as many people as they could possibly reach. They revolutionised the church by the simple expedient of going outside the church buildings and preaching in public. Wesley became the leader of the main Methodist movement and for half a century set about reshaping the spiritual landscape in Britain. Wesley had a passion for the poor. He made every effort to reach the working poor and to draw them into Methodism. He also greatly encouraged Methodists to reach out and care for the most destitute and needy people in the nation—prisoners, the homeless, the illiterate, alcoholics. However, the really significant thing about Methodism was its attempt to enable the poor to be an integral part of the movement. Anyone who professed faith in Christ, however poor and uneducated, was invited to the weekly 'class' meetings[17] (or 'Band Societies') in which members shared their lives together and challenged and supported each other to live truly godly lives. These meetings were no mere middle class talking shops and social clubs—they were practical, prayerful and simple. Methodist classes were open to the poor and became the nurturing ground for generations of those in need who embraced the Christian faith. Here they found that they were equal before God and part of a supportive fellowship that could help them navigate the huge challenges of their relatively impoverished lives.

The genius of the Methodist 'class' system was that these groups were easy for the working class poor to join. There were usually about twelve members in a group who all committed themselves to meet weekly and to discuss basic and personal questions about their spiritual welfare and their daily lives.[18] It was a supportive accountability group. Members did not need education, money or a strong position in society to attend. They did not have to be able to read or to talk confidently. Everyone came in as equals who were there to share their lives openly and simply in the light of their common Christian faith. The class meetings subverted the social hierarchy of the day. They helped to set the spiritual and relational DNA of the Methodist movement and formed its backbone many years before it started to establish separate Sunday church congregations.

By the time of Wesley's death in 1791 Methodism had established itself as a potent renewal movement in the church. Its influence grew steadily as the nineteenth century unfolded and a broader evangelical movement gained momentum. This was a movement that was in evidence in many different types of church and organisations. The eighteenth century Methodist spiritual awakening had indeed sparked a major renewal in the churches that could be observed in denominations as diverse as the Quakers, the Church of England, Methodism itself, the Baptists and then, later, the Salvation Army. One outworking of this influence was political and social activism and the adoption of many causes such as anti-slavery, prison reform and educational development. However, what is vital to note for our purposes is that the values of Methodism included a significant commitment to be a church for the poor. This commitment influenced subsequent churches and movements. It was a process that continued into the twentieth century and up to our own time through movements such as the Welsh Revival and Pentecostalism.

I want to suggest three insights that come from a knowledge of the church history of this period.

Spiritual renewal has often led to efforts to build a church for the poor

Where the Methodists had led, others followed—directly or indirectly. Let's look at a few significant examples.

Charles Spurgeon

Charles Spurgeon, the famous Baptist pastor, was reputed to be the greatest preacher of the nineteenth-century evangelical movement. For three decades he led the largest church in the UK at the time— the Metropolitan Tabernacle in London. In his early years as a preacher there was an extraordinary sense of spiritual renewal accompanying his sermons, which led to a swift gathering of thousands of followers to become his congregation. However,

Spurgeon was more than a preacher and an evangelist. He was also concerned for the poor. He founded orphanages and sponsored numerous initiatives to help those in need. Equally significantly, he also focused on church planting—especially in the poorer districts of London. Under his inspiration and leadership the number of Baptist churches in London more than doubled in the second half of the nineteenth century and many new churches were planted specifically in order to reach the working poor and the marginalised across London.

Spurgeon had a city-wide vision for London and a genuine heart for the poor. He wanted to plant churches in poor neighbourhoods. He founded the Pastor's College (later Spurgeon's College) in south London and used it to train, envision and send numerous young men to be church-planters across the city (and beyond). He often visited the most deprived areas of London and he encouraged church planters in those areas to find suitable ways to reach the poor.

The Salvation Army

William Booth was a Methodist, steeped in the history of Methodism. However, he felt that the Methodist church of his day was not radical enough in reaching the poor; it had become too middle class for his liking. So he and his wife founded the Salvation Army in 1865. Booth aimed to reach the poor directly—initially in the east end of London. His early catchphrase was 'The Three 'S's', expressing the way in which the Salvation Army reached out to the 'down and outs': first, soup; second, soap; and finally, salvation. Booth passionately believed that the best way to help the poor was to teach them the Christian gospel and invite them to accept Christ by faith. However, he equally strongly believed in the need to provide practical help to those in poverty. He set about energetically to achieve both these goals—and with considerable success. The first converts were mostly alcoholics, prostitutes, homeless or the otherwise 'undesirables' of society. The Salvation Army grew in numbers and influence very rapidly at the end of the nineteenth century. Their consistent aim was to reach out to the poorest in every community in which they established a new 'corps'—or church.

The Salvation Army managed to present the Christian message in a way that appealed directly to the poor. Salvationists came to their communities and jettisoned the cultural context of the middle-class church in favour of a more ground-level type of church culture. The military style structure gave poor people something to belong to and a 'war' to believe in. The use of music hall tunes enhanced the hymns. The populist and practical preaching appealed to the heart and was easy to understand. Here was a church culture birthed in a mission to the poor. Early converts did not feel that they were joining a middle-class church—they felt the Salvation Army was their own, part of their own culture.

The Welsh Revival

The Welsh Revival of 1904-1905 was a sudden spiritual awakening that quickly spread in influence across Wales, then into the rest of the UK and beyond. Tens of thousands were drawn into the chapels of Wales in a very short time. There was no single organisation or leader behind the revival, although it was strongly associated with its best-known preacher, Evan Roberts. Roberts was a working-class man who started his working life in the mines of south Wales. The Welsh Revival was consciously a movement of the working poor. Roberts geared his preaching to the culture of the working man and woman. Miners, factory workers, farm labourers and shop-workers mingled together in huge numbers in the Welsh chapels during and after the revival years. To a great extent, this concern for the working poor was also evident in the early Pentecostal Apostolic and Elim movements that emerged from Wales in the years following the Welsh Revival.

Building a church for the poor has required new strategies for church life and mission

Not many leaders were willing to be as radical as William Booth, whose Salvation Army church communities were deliberately geared towards the poor. This was done through direct and dramatic evangelism—street preaching, public hall events, special music and clothing, billboard advertising and the like. Booth believed that the institution of the local church had to look and feel significantly different in order to attract and keep those facing poverty. The Salvation Army's straightforward liturgy, direct preaching style, military culture and clear ethical teachings were all designed to be accessible to converts from poorer parts of Victorian society.

An alternative approach was that of strategic and intentional church planting. This is what Spurgeon advocated, as we saw above.

Spurgeon's own city centre church remained largely attended by the middle classes of Victorian London, but he used the resources of his huge church and the training college he had founded to open the way for church planting in the poorer districts of London. Spurgeon was not alone in adopting this strategy. Churches as different as the Brethren and the high Anglican churches sought to establish congregations in poorer parts of the growing Victorian towns and cities.

A slight modification of church planting was the concept of the 'Mission Hall', which grew up across the UK in the nineteenth century. Denominational churches or mission agencies built and staffed halls for outreach purposes in many poorer housing estates and inner city areas. This was sometimes done as estates were being built, but alternatively the church moved in to an unchurched poor area by setting up a Mission Hall. External financial support was usually forthcoming for such halls, which often flourished for a time. However, they rarely had the status of churches in their own right and tended to fall into decline over time. Many have closed in recent years.

New Testament teaching has provided the strongest stimulus in building a church for the poor

We have commented briefly on different church leaders, initiatives and contexts. We have looked at differing methodologies. We have noticed the significance of spiritual renewal as an impetus to seeking to build a church for the poor. However, there is one factor that stands out as a uniting theme when it comes to building a church for the poor. This factor is the power of the New Testament itself. All the leaders and movements we have mentioned took their primary inspiration from a careful study of the New Testament. They were willing to rethink the church traditions they grew up with in the light of the New Testament. In the previous chapter we looked at how the New Testament writings indicate the priority of reaching the poor. Wesley found this vision compelling. So did Spurgeon, and Booth—and countless others who helped build a church for the poor during past centuries in the UK.

So what about us?

There has been a significant spiritual renewal happening in the church in the UK since the 1960s through the advent of the 'charismatic movement'. I have lived through it and experienced most of its phases and emphases. Looking back over half a century of this renewal movement we can see some huge changes and positive developments. Here are just a few that come to mind: changing worship patterns; a huge increase in lay ministry; the strengthening of the community of the church; the wider use of spiritual gifts; the development of team leadership patterns; the emergence of significant evangelistic ministries; the foundation of hundreds of 'new churches'—the list could go on.

However, there's one thing missing. We haven't yet rediscovered a vision to build a church for the poor. We have engaged with social action and that is a good thing. But there is a step more.

There are pioneers out there who have been captured by this vision, but their work is not yet part of the mainstream of UK church culture. This needs to change, and in order to make that change we need to know the culture we're working in.

FIVE

BRITISH CULTURE: DIVIDING WALLS

We started this book with the story of Julie, who came to my (Natalie's) church in need, came to faith in Jesus, but then after a while drifted back to her old lifestyle. As we travel across the UK, speaking with Christians from churches of various denominations, two of the most common questions we are asked are: firstly, how do we keep people from poorer and working class backgrounds (and these aren't necessarily the same thing, as we will see below) in the church? And secondly, how do we integrate people from those backgrounds into our mainly middle class churches?

Part of the problem is that it's difficult for us to think from the perspective of someone who has had a completely different life experience. I mentioned that I used to feel a great deal of anxiety when invited to someone's house for dinner. Lately, I've talked to friends about that a lot, and nine times out of ten the response is: 'I never would have thought about that.' Some of us are so used to going to dinner with friends that it doesn't even cross our minds that others may feel less comfortable in that setting. I'd been a Christian for over ten years and attended countless dinners and parties at people's houses before a friend took me to one side to tell me that it's polite to bring a bottle of drink when you're invited to someone's house. I had no idea that was 'the done thing'. I'm grateful someone told me, but I wonder why it took a decade, and I wonder how many people noticed but didn't say anything.

Class attitudes and divisions

As I've seen others from a working class or poorer background come and go from church life in my own setting, I have often wondered if the fact that I have stuck around is due, in part, to my ability to adapt to middle class behaviour: I found it relatively easy to observe how others around me acted and to mimic that until it came naturally to me. (I'm not saying that it hasn't been because of God's sovereignty and work in my life—of course it has!—but I cannot help but wonder what held me in church life when many others with a background similar to mine have found it so difficult to feel at home in the church community.)

I was recently talking to one of the former leaders of my church about the difficulty in connecting people from working class or poor backgrounds into church life. I commented that we don't seem to be able to help them to effectively integrate and thereby remain in the church community long-term in the same way we are able to help middle class people do this. He was surprised I thought this was the case—he was able to name several people who are currently in my church who came into the church around twenty years ago from working class backgrounds. As we talked, he pointed out that I didn't know where they'd come from and, because they're very middle class now, I assumed they always had been. But, like me, over many years they had changed. The church leader remarked that they had been so transformed 'you might never guess what they were like when they first became Christians'. He was right. With most of those he named, I would not have known anything of their working class roots.

There are often still some tell-tale signs, obviously. A different church leader has confessed that he judged my intellect and academic ability based on my accent when he first met me a few years ago. He was shocked when, a few minutes into the conversation, I mentioned that I was about to start studying for my master's degree in political communication. Despite my background and my accent, I am now middle class in almost every way, and in my case that is largely due to becoming a Christian, copying the behaviour of others in church life, and aspiring for different things for my life as a result.

Is this why our churches are so middle class? In his book *Chav Christianity*,[19] Darren Edwards explores this in detail, reflecting on the fact that often when someone from a working class background becomes a Christian, they are encouraged to move to a nicer area, get their children into a better school, build up some savings, and so on. There is nothing necessarily wrong with that. But Edwards points out that if every working class Christian becomes culturally middle class, our churches become full of middle class people and there are no working class Christians left in communities where other working class people live. Instead, he argues that those who are working class should be free to be themselves, not pushed to conform to middle class standards.

This is an interesting provocation for three clear reasons. Firstly, the majority of British people still describe themselves as working class.[20] We may feel like our society has moved beyond class issues—perhaps we look back to the era of an 'upstairs, downstairs' divide between the wealthy and their servants and think such vivid class distinctions are behind us. It's been a century since the vote was given to those who don't own their own homes and almost twenty years since then-Prime Minister Tony Blair set himself on a mission to remove the 'old class divisions'. The proportion of people in typically working class jobs is now estimated to be just a quarter of the British workforce. Yet 60 percent of British people still identify themselves as culturally working class, according to the 2015 British Social Attitudes Survey—a figure that has not changed since 1983. Significantly, 82 percent of those who describe themselves as working class feel that there is a wide divide between social classes, and 76 percent believe it is difficult to move from one class to another. (Actually, 71 percent of those who identify as middle class also think it's difficult to move from one class to another.) Based on the data, the authors of the 33rd British Social Attitudes Survey conclude: 'Working class identity remains widespread in Britain. Even though only a minority of people are engaged in working class occupations, a majority of us still think of ourselves as working class.'[21]

The second reason it is important for us to reflect on class issues is because the truly working class are woefully under-represented in British churches. A Tearfund report in 2007 found

that church-going is 'a middle class pursuit', with adult professionals and managers being more likely to attend church regularly than
skilled, semi-skilled, and unskilled manual workers.[22] Interestingly,
those who are (for whatever reason) entirely dependent on the
state are the most likely to not be currently attending church but
most open to attending in the future. A more recent YouGov
survey, conducted in 2014, found that 62 percent of people who
regularly attend church identify as middle class, while only 38
percent identify as working class.[23] More surprisingly, *Talking Jesus*
research, conducted in 2015, found that 81 percent of practising
Christians in Britain today have a university degree.[24] This
compares to around 27 percent in the population as a whole.[25] So
the demographics in our churches do not reflect the demographics
in our communities. We are missing a large section of society.

Thirdly, the gospel is not middle class. Jesus engaged with
people across every social stratum—the rich, the powerful, the
impoverished, the despised, the isolated—yet was very clear that
the gospel was especially good news to the poor, as we have already
seen. He said: 'Blessed are you who are poor, for yours is the
kingdom of God. Blessed are you who hunger now, for you will be
satisfied' (Luke 6:20-21) and, as we saw earlier, there is a promise
to 'those who are poor in the eyes of the world' that God has
chosen them 'to be rich in faith and to inherit the kingdom' (James
2:5).

So, to recap what we have discovered so far in this chapter:
Class is still a significant issue in British society. A majority of
people in Britain today identify as working class—even if some of
them are economically indistinguishable from many middle class

people. Only 38 percent of people in our churches identify as working class, however, and the true working class are really not well represented at all. The working class—and indeed the middle class—believe it is difficult for people to move from one class to another. The gospel is not reserved for the middle class but is especially good news for the poor.

This poses a significant challenge for our churches, yet many of us live our day-to-day lives without thinking about how class affects us. The reality is that our background and our experiences provide a lens through which we see the world around us, and there are clear class distinctions that shape our perspectives. It is not just that we have different tastes and preferences, but that we are often starting from a different place entirely. Dr Ruby Payne outlines this in her book *A Framework for Understanding Poverty*, by showing different attitudes people have to food: someone from a working class or poorer background is most likely to be concerned with quantity—did you have enough?—whereas for the middle class person, quality—did you like it?—is the key question. Likewise with thinking about money and time. Surviving in the present will be the more important factor to someone facing poverty or struggling to make ends meet. Saving for the future is a key value and aspiration for the middle class. Dr Payne explores the driving forces of the different classes. She concludes that relationships and entertainment motivate and are important to the working class or poor, whereas work and achievement drive the middle classes.[26]

Differing outlooks between classes have been evidently at work in recent British history, with the success of the 'leave' vote in the referendum of 2016 on whether Britain should remain in the European Union being attributed largely to class differences. While the majority of the AB group (professionals and managers) voted to remain in the EU, two-thirds of the C2DE (working class) group voted to leave. Lines could be drawn by various class indicators, including educational attainment, home-ownership and employment status.[27] (As a noteworthy aside: I know of a number of Christians who posted on social media in the immediate aftermath of the referendum statements such as 'people should have to pass an IQ test before they vote', which betrays a shocking attitude to people 'not like us'.

Races and racism

Everything we have explored so far in this chapter could be said to mainly focus on the white working class in Britain. However, black and ethnic minority communities in Britain are far more likely to experience poverty than white British people. In London, for example, in the three years up to 2013/14, 58 percent of those originally from Bangladesh and Pakistan and 49 percent of black Africans were in poverty, compared with just 17 percent of their white British neighbours.[28] Similarly, in 2014 black people living in London were most likely to be unemployed—11 percent compared to 4 percent of white British Londoners—and most likely to be sanctioned by the Job Centre.[29] For the nation as a whole, the statistics are similar, with the poverty rate being consistently lowest among white British people and those who are black or black British being twice as likely to experience poverty.[30]

Race is hugely relevant to poverty in Britain today and therefore vitally important when contemplating how to build a church for the poor. I was recently privy to a conversation between two people in church leadership—a black man and a white woman—about the use of the hashtag #blacklivesmatter in the wake of another shooting in America. There was debate about the alternative hashtag #alllivesmatter, and my black friend—Ben Lindsay, who leads a church plant in London—explained why, from his perspective, that hashtag was missing the point. He explained that the reason why the #blacklivesmatter hashtag matters is because of the historic racism and brutality that the minority culture in America has suffered from the majority culture. Ben said: 'This has had various expressions, resulting in a consistent devaluation of black lives over centuries. #Alllivesmatter is a kick in the teeth because historically some lives have been valued more than others, which is why it's important to now say black lives matter. It's a matter of justice.'

Ben also outlined how important it is that white people speak up on race issues. I confessed that, as a white woman, I'm afraid to do so because I'm not sure if it would be seen as patronising, or if I'd get it wrong somehow. He pointed out that from a black perspective, when white friends and colleagues do not speak up, it can look like consent, apathy and a lack of empathy. It may not be that, but that is how it can be interpreted: that the majority culture does not care about the suffering of the minority. This means that all the time white people don't speak out—whether through fear or some other reason—segregation and separation continues, and we all become further entrenched in our own groups.

When it comes to our churches, in the same way that middle class people need to actively seek to understand those from a working class background and vice versa, so we also need to spend time with people from different cultures. It is the only way we will break down dividing walls and build churches that reflect a New Testament picture of the church. This requires honest conversations, pointing out where we may have inadvertently caused offence by not understanding cultural differences. But as Ben points out, this is only possible if we're building strong relationships with people from different backgrounds, where we can have robust discussions about how we might be offending one another and those around us.

We also need to ensure we are not speaking about inclusivity without putting it into practice. It is one thing to say that we believe all people are equal before God, but another to create a level playing field where people from all backgrounds have the same opportunities. Ben highlights this by saying that if a white, middle class leader stands up on a Sunday and says to the congregation that we want a diverse, inclusive church, but doesn't ever invite anyone from an ethnic minority or working class or poor background to dinner at his house, we have to ask some questions about how important inclusivity really is. Likewise, if members of our churches only see a certain type of person on the platform—if our preachers and worship leaders and youth team are all white, middle class and married, for example—then no matter what we say about diversity and all being equal, we will be communicating something very different to those who are not white, not middle class, and not married.

Another factor to consider is that we must listen to individual stories so that we avoid stereotypes and assumptions. Ben mentioned the story of a black woman in his church who had a very privileged education and subsequently felt she had more in common with fairly affluent white people in the church than any other group, yet felt 'put in a box' by church members who expected her to mainly relate to other black people. So while bearing in mind that poverty is more likely to affect people who are not white British, we need to also be mindful that for many people of other ethnicities this will not be their experience at all. That is one reason why we must take time to get to know people, to invest in them and to understand their culture or subculture if we're to build a church where all people feel welcome, included and at home.

The issue of rural poverty

The discussion of poverty is almost always focused on urban contexts. This is understandable but it does not present a complete picture. Rural poverty needs to be considered. It is a reality—although often conveniently located in remote and apparently insignificant places.

My (Martin's) church is set in a market town in the middle of a very rural county, Shropshire. Our church serves people across a wide rural area beyond our town and we support other churches located in villages and small towns across the area as they reach out to the poorest members of their communities.

Rural poverty is hidden poverty. People tend to live far apart from each other. Small enclaves of social housing can be more or less unnoticed to the casual observer or passing visitor. However, the reality is that there are many rural dumping grounds for people in difficult circumstances who are placed there because of lack of housing capacity in urban areas. Affluent villagers can turn a blind eye to the social issues that are represented in these small housing enclaves nearby. People can live in parallel worlds all too easily.

A particular issue in rural areas is the relative weakness of local churches. Many are in numerical decline and fighting for survival. Many are filled with elderly congregations. Many lack paid church leaders. Many lack social vision and a desire to reach out effectively to the nearby pockets of poverty. There are exceptions, of course. However, the overall situation means that many of the rural poor are effectively out of the reach of churches near to them.

Rural poverty has a few specific aspects which deserve comment. Firstly, transport is a big issue. Bus services are in decline in most rural areas and the cost of maintaining cars is greater in the countryside due to longer journeys to key amenities and poor roads in some areas. Secondly, digital exclusion is sometimes higher in rural areas due to local culture and unreliable broadband. Thirdly, access to key amenities is often more difficult. A trip to a low-cost supermarket can be a major commitment of time and transport cost. The same can be said for medical facilities, libraries, jobcentres and other important amenities.

The rural poor can easily be ignored by the church. The strong churches are mostly in suburban areas. If they have a sense of outreach to the poor it will probably be directed towards nearby deprived urban communities. The rural poor can be forgotten or marginalised in a little-recognised social division between town and country. The church will perpetuate this division unless it strives deliberately to overcome it by finding creative ways of reaching out to the rural poor.

Conclusion

The gospel presents a stark contrast to the divisions we see in our communities. We may feel like we don't know how to cross boundaries of ethnicity or class, or even a rural/urban divide, or we may not even be contemplating how to cross them. In the kingdom of God, barriers are broken down, dividing walls of hostility are removed, and all people groups can be reconciled in Christ (see Eph. 2:11-22, Gal. 3:28, 1 Peter 2:9-11, Phil. 3:20, Col. 3:11, etc.). Ultimately we know that God's people will comprise every tribe, nation and tongue (Rev. 7:9)—surely that includes people from every class too!

The problem is that we are all shaped by our own cultural norms on such a deep level that it is hard for us to see it. It is often not until someone says something that jolts us out of our own understanding that we realise how much we have been influenced by what we consider to be normal. For example, a church leader told me (Natalie) recently that when she had invited a working class couple from the church to dinner with her and her husband, their response was: 'Why? What have we done?' Until this point, it hadn't occurred to her that a dinner invitation could be interpreted in this way. When I heard this story I realised how middle class I have become—I had forgotten that my parents never went to other people's houses for dinner when I was growing up. They were in and out of neighbours' homes sharing cups of tea and gossip about the street, yes, but going to friends' houses for dinner was simply not something I had seen adults do until I became a Christian.

The point is that some of the things that seem so normal and natural to us are very foreign and strange to other people. But it takes effort for us to realise this. We have to intentionally ponder such things and talk to people openly and honestly. Otherwise we will put up barriers without even realising it. In the context of church life, this might mean we need to rethink how we do mid-week life (it isn't 'normal' for people from all social groups to go out in the evenings during the week). We will need to think about our preaching—not just what language we're using and how long we're preaching, but also the illustrations we use and the style of communicating. A working class church leader I know pointed out to a group of mainly middle class leaders that when during a sermon we publicly mock people who read *The Sun*, that smug sense of superiority can't be expected to win over anyone who might, in fact, read *The Sun*. An obvious point, yet one we can so easily miss. Even some of our social action projects can wildly miss the mark: I was involved in running three budgeting courses in my church before I realised a major reason we were only attracting Christians to them was because we held them at 7.30pm on a mid-week evening. Had I listened sooner to some of the people we wanted to come along and expected to benefit from them, I would have realised this time wasn't going to serve them well.

We need to break down these barriers so that our churches can increasingly reflect the kingdom of God. But in order to do that, we need to reflect on some of the attitudes in our hearts that might prevent our churches from more accurately reflecting our society and welcoming people from all demographics, without expecting them to transition from one social group to another.

SIX

BRITISH CULTURE: MATERIALISM, INDIVIDUALISM, CYNICISM

'God wants you to have nice things,' a friend said to me (Natalie) as I was about to move into the flat I had just bought—my first home of my own. The comment stayed with me for weeks. I struggled to work out if it is true, or if it is just something it's easy for us Christians living in wealthy, Western societies to tell ourselves to justify our comfort. If it is true, I cannot easily back up this idea from the Bible. A careful reading of the New Testament makes clear that both Jesus and members of the early church sought to live lives of material simplicity in which their main focus was on advancing God's kingdom, not acquiring unnecessary material goods for the sake of a comfortable life. I know that Jesus promised that God would take care of our essential needs—specifically mentioning food, drink and clothing (Luke 12:22-34), but I am not convinced he is particularly concerned about whether or not I have 'nice things' such as the latest smartphone or an expensive sofa.

It is not necessarily wrong to have money and 'nice things'. It is possible to be wealthy and not materialistic, or indeed poor and very materialistic. But my friend's statement caused me to reflect on my own materialism, and how much I have bought into one of the entrenched attitudes of British culture. Nationwide's Christmas Spending Report, released a few days before Christmas 2016, predicted that people in the UK would spend £33 billion on Christmas that year, with 30 percent of us getting into debt and 19 percent suffering financially for three or more months as a result.[31] The same report said that 37 percent of us would later regret how much we spent on Christmas. So why do we do it?

We live in a society where it is now normal and common to spend money that is not ours. This is a new aspect of our culture that simply did not exist in the era before credit cards. It is important to remember how new and unusual this reality is. Credit cards appeared in the UK in the 1960s and today most people pay by card for at least half of what they buy.[32] Previously people had to save up before making expensive purchases; now we can put them on a card and pay them off over months or even years. This has led to a dramatic and ongoing rise in personal indebtedness over the past few decades. In March 2017, individuals in the UK owed more than £1.5 trillion, with the average debt per UK adult at £30,105 including mortgages—114 percent of average earnings—and on average one person becoming insolvent every six minutes in England and Wales.[33] Citizens Advice Bureaux in England and Wales are dealing with more than 4,000 debt problems every single day.[34]

Research by the Charities Aid Foundation in 2014 found that 73 percent of Britons think the UK is becoming more materialistic. Fifty-nine percent think we are too focused on our own lives to help others, and that we are more likely to spend more on holidays, clothes, leisure and eating out/takeaways than on giving to good causes.[35]

It might be easy for Christians to imagine we are untouched by the materialism and consumerism that surrounds us. Perhaps when we look at escalating spending and debt, we can feel that we are free of the love of money so evident in our society. If we steward our money well, don't borrow unnecessarily, and are committed to saving, then we are okay, aren't we? It is important to make a sober assessment of ourselves in this area.

There has been a growing movement in some parts of the church in recent years advocating what we might call the principle of 'simplicity' in our material lives. The American author Richard Foster popularised this concept in the 1980s with his classic book *The Freedom of Simplicity*.[36] Many others have followed in his path in a theological and practical critique of materialism. The principle of simplicity demands that we always question whether material things are strictly necessary or truly useful to us as we seek to be Jesus' disciples. Such questioning can lead to major changes in priorities and economic decisions. If the pursuit of simplicity is combined with a commitment to radical generosity, then we quickly begin to find freedom from slavish adherence to the demands of materialism and a greater release of resources for the work of the kingdom of God.

A very challenging example of the outworking of the principle of simplicity in a past era was John Wesley. His story is worth telling again.

Wesley once gave away ninety-eight percent of his annual income. I can think I'm doing well when I give anything above ten percent! We live in an easy-credit society that encourages people to live beyond their means. As Christians, we can feel counter-cultural simply by living *according* to our means, but spending more just because you earn more isn't a kingdom principle.

Wesley, one of the greatest preachers and theologians of the eighteenth century, was moved by God to consider how much of his income he could give away to the poor. He began to limit his expenses when he was twenty-eight and earning £30 per year. He worked out that he could live on £28, so he gave away £2.

The next year, his income doubled but he continued to live as he had before, giving away £32. Likewise, when his income went up to £90 in the third year, he was still able to live on the same amount and give away the surplus £62.

He hit a peak of £1,400 in one year, yet he gave away all of it except £30.

Wesley died in 1791 at the age of 87. The only money mentioned in his will was 'the miscellaneous coins to be found in his pockets and dresser drawers'.[37]

Challenging, isn't it? And it is relevant to how we build a church for the poor because if we are not careful we can see the acquisition of possessions and our own comfort as more important than generosity to those around us. Does God want me to have 'nice things'? Maybe. But I have felt challenged over the last few years to consider if it is right for me to have considerably more than I need while there are people around me who do not have everything they need in order to live viably in our society.

Materialism can be an obstacle to building a church for the poor because it can hinder our generosity and cause others to feel that they need to attain a certain standard of living to 'fit in' with the culture of our churches. It can keep us preoccupied with our own comfort and distract us from those around us in need. Ultimately, if we let it take root in our lives, it can make our possessions more valuable to us than people. Here are three specific ways in which materialism hinders our capacity to build a church for the poor:

Materialism—less money for the kingdom of God

Firstly, it takes our money and channels it into acquiring more, rather than sharing it and helping others. When we spend more, we obviously have less capacity to give, whether that is to people around us, to our churches or to charities or projects supporting those who have less than us. I became keenly aware of this as I planned to buy my home—I wondered why the mortgage lender felt the repayments would be easy for me, when I thought they might stretch me financially. My church leader said, 'It is because they don't assume you give money away.' I realised that taking on this extra expense, legitimate though it may be, would leave me less disposable income, and a greater temptation to trim what I give away. I would therefore need to be very intentional about continuing to grow in generosity. One paradox of many churches is this—some of the richer members often give very little to the church. Pastors often puzzle over this fact. It is a matter of quiet discussion among trustees and treasurers. The explanation is usually quite simple. For many richer people, as their income goes up, their outgoings and financial commitments go up at the same rate. Greater income can mean a bigger house, an extension, more exotic holidays, bigger cars, etc. as we endeavour to fit in with the culture around us. But the Bible says: 'Command those who are rich in this present world [...] to do good, to be rich in good deeds, and to be generous and willing to share' (1 Tim. 6:17-18). Wesley was able to give away so much of what he had because he identified with and aspired to be part of the church on the ground.

Materialism—less time for the kingdom of God

However, materialism does not just take our money; it also takes our time. If we are preoccupied with what we have, we will have less time to think about serving others. We will also need to spend more time earning money so that we can live up to the standards to which we have become accustomed. A Unicef report published by the United Nations in 2011 backs this up. According to John Humphrys, reviewing the report for YouGov, it found:

> British parents spend too little time with their children because they are working too hard, and then try to compensate by showering their kids with toys and designer-labelled clothes. But this, the report says, is pointless because such consumer goods are not what make children happy.
>
> This new research was commissioned after an earlier Unicef report concluded that Britain was the worst country among twenty one developed countries for children to grow up in.[38]

Humphrys goes on to note that British children said that time with their family is what most makes them happy, yet it seems to be in short supply. When we are committed to acquiring more and more money and possessions, we do not have as much time to invest in the people around us. This can also be evidenced by the impact of materialism on relationships: one study published by the *Journal of Couple & Relationship Therapy* found that it has a negative impact on happiness in marriages even when both people are materialistic.[39] When we're preoccupied with wealth, we are also likely to invest more of our time in wealth-dependent leisure activities, leaving us less time for the kingdom of God.

Materialism—less creative energy for the kingdom of God

In addition to siphoning away our money and time, materialism uses up our creative energy, which instead goes on building up our affluent lifestyles and recreation activities, which can in turn consume all the available creative energy of many a church member. It is a danger to consider. Such people turn up on Sundays in spiritual need, keen to receive what the church can offer, but with little to give to the church community in terms of creative energy—or energy full stop. Often just a little personal reflection and reconsideration of lifestyle issues can make all the difference in this respect.

In my church, I (Martin) have a reputation for seeking out church members who are planning to retire soon. I usually try to have a meeting with them in the year before their retirement, in which I quietly mention a few key areas of church life to which the shortly to be retired church members might be able to contribute. Very often they are persuaded to give some of their new-found time and creative energy to church projects—especially social action projects!

It is important that Christians take the time to explore whether materialism has taken root in our lives. We only have to ask ourselves what we cannot go a day or a week without, or how we feel when someone asks if they can borrow our car, for example, to spot if there is a flicker of this in our own hearts. For some of us it may not be that we are committed to building up our money and possessions, but that a sober assessment reveals we are simply more committed to our comfort than we are to God's kingdom. That may sound harsh, but if I (Natalie) am truly honest, I see it in my own heart often. The way to keep a check on it is to seek God, frequently asking him to pinpoint anything we own that is actually owning us, and any attitudes that have crept in from the culture around us.

The power of individualism

Just as we can be shaped by our background in terms of class and our culture in terms of materialism, we also run the risk of being affected by the rampant individualism we see in our society. A 2009 study found that Britain was the most individualistic country in the world: 'one that valued the self over the group more than any other country'.[40]

Again, we might feel that as Christians we are impervious to the individualism around us, but we do not have to look too hard to see it in our churches. In recent years there has been an emphasis on finding personal fulfilment in our Christian lives through an emphasis on God's personal love, plan and purpose for each believer. This is not bad in and of itself, but we must remember that we are part of the body of Christ. We have not been saved for a relationship with God alone, but to be a reflection of him to those around us, both inside and outside the church. We are part of something bigger than ourselves. God's plan is to build us together—each one of us equally valuable to him. He is preparing a bride for his Son, formed of people from every nation, tribe and tongue. Jesus' second greatest commandment is that we are to love our neighbours as we love ourselves. There is no place in the church for the kind of individualism we see in our society, but we need to be intentional about rooting it out. Cultural concerns with personal space and boundaries may have influenced us in ways that we are not even aware of. Some other cultures are known for prioritising the community above the individual, which often includes acts of sacrifice and selflessness. British society is not known for this.

Both materialism and individualism separate us from people who are different to us. We have mentioned already that in our previous book, *The Myth of the Undeserving Poor*, we found that our proximity to people in need affects what we think about poverty in Britain today.[41] Materialism and individualism both make us more selfish and less likely to spend time with people who have less than us, because both cause us to focus on ourselves. This is damaging and prohibits us from building a church for the poor, because we are less likely to have meaningful engagement with people who don't have what we have, and who may require more from us (materially, emotionally and spiritually) than we are prepared to give.

The impact of cynicism

A further reason this is a problem is because of another facet of British culture: our tendency towards cynicism and tearing others down. We see this play out in the media all the time. The slightest mistake or error in judgement from a politician or celebrity or anyone in the public eye is paraded for all to see and comment on. For over thirty years Ipsos-MORI has carried out its 'trust survey', demonstrating how little the British public trust politicians, journalists, bankers, clergy and more. Their 2016 survey showed a clear difference between generations, with 56 percent of those born between 1980 and 2000 trusting the average person to tell the truth, compared to 68 percent of Generation X (born 1966-1979), 75 percent of Baby Boomers (1945-65) and 78 percent of the Pre-War generation (before 1945).

This cynicism and distrust of others has contributed to our sense that people make their own success or failure—that 'good people' do well in life and those who struggle are architects of their own circumstances. This is the premise of the American dream—that anyone who works hard will eventually enjoy success and achieve whatever they hope for. We can so easily buy into the narrative that those who work hard prosper and those who don't, don't. But the Bible doesn't see it as this clear cut. There are numerous verses about bad things happening to those who do right and the wicked prospering. Job is a classic example of a good, hard-working man losing all he has and finding himself in desperate need through no fault of his own. Of course, working hard is good and right, and the Bible doesn't shy away from the fact that often people do end up in dire straits through their own decision-making (see the prodigal son, for example). But we cannot assume that everyone who does well deserves their success and everyone who is poor has made their own bed.

This kind of cynicism can so easily prevent us from helping those in need. If we allow it to take root, we find ourselves quickly writing off entire groups of people, whether it is those on benefits or immigrants or any other group we may find it hard to identify with. Yet it is incredibly easy for us to fall into a cynical attitude of heart, especially when we are let down by people we help. We can feel a crushing sense of disappointment when someone we've helped makes the same bad decisions again or becomes a Christian but then wanders off. We can find ourselves outraged when someone seems to just want to take more and more from us, or it transpires they were taking advantage of us all along. Things such as these happen often when we seriously invest our time and energy in building churches for the poor. We have to guard our hearts so that the disappointment we rightly feel doesn't turn into a cynicism that wrongly hardens us to others.

As Christians we are called to see the best in people–to acknowledge their sin and brokenness, but to recognise the image of God in the person in front of us, believing the best for them, and not giving up on people when it gets tough. We might need to apply different strategies and ensure we're being wise, but God's mercy towards us has never been based on what we do or fail to do. Likewise, our kindness to people around us shouldn't be based on how they treat us but on how Jesus has treated us. In the kingdom of God, kindness, compassion and generosity have everything to do with the giver and very little to do with the recipient. There's no place for cynicism in the Christian. Wisdom, yes. But let's not mistake the two.

Conclusion

Christians are to be counter-cultural in all of these areas. Where there is a focus on material possessions, we are to point to eternal treasures that cannot spoil or fade. Where there is individualism, we are to seek the good of those around us and our communities as a whole. And where there is cynicism and negativity towards people (individuals or groups), we are to bring hope and encouragement, recognising every person as someone who bears the image of God and can reflect something of his character to others. Only by going against the grain of British culture in these areas, can we build churches that really are homes for those who are poor or in need.

Our culture is a key filter that influences the way we see the world around us. Materialism, individualism and cynicism are all key parts of that filter in British culture today. This cultural filter can easily distort how we see our salvation—focusing too much on the personal benefits it gives us. It can distort how we see the church—focusing too much on using our churches to meet our own personal needs. And our cultural filter can also dramatically impact how we see the poor and needy. It can disguise the significance of the vast gap in standards of living that are present in our country. It can distance us from real personal engagement with the poor. It can take away resources that could be deployed for the church to reach the poor. Finally, and most importantly, it can prevent us having a vision for the UK church to be a church for the poor.

SEVEN

HEART RESPONSE

For *The Myth of the Undeserving Poor*, we carried out research into what shapes the views of Christians when it comes to poverty in Britain today.[42] The results showed, in a nutshell, that we are just as susceptible to being shaped by the media we read or watch as we are by what we read in the Bible. We also found that our perspectives on poverty are connected to our political preferences and to our proximity to those in poverty.

We reflected on the fact that it's easy for us to believe that we're impervious to these external factors, but biblically speaking we know that what we spend time meditating on and thinking about has the power to mould us. It is why we're instructed to think about things that are noble, praiseworthy and true (Phil. 4:8), take our thoughts captive (2 Cor. 10:5) and renew our minds (Rom. 12:2). It's why reading the Bible and dwelling on the truth is important. Most of us will know from experience that when we spend time thinking about things that are not true, such as things that have been said to us about ourselves, it doesn't take long for them to seep into us and require significant attention and effort to root out.

It is no different with what we read in newspapers or watch on TV. As we explored in detail in *The Myth of the Undeserving Poor*, some of the media narratives around poverty in Britain today are damaging and foster prejudice, causing us to fear people who are not like us. In academic circles, this is called 'conflictual framing' or 'othering'. It pits 'us' against 'them', exacerbating our differences and pushing us farther apart from people we already may not understand.

In British society today, it is very difficult not to buy into the media and political narrative that those in poverty are to blame for their plight. Examples of 'skivers' are paraded in front of us through headlines such as 'Half a million scroungers get benefits ... and you pay'[43] and through television programmes such as *Benefits Street*. There is a mix of British stoicism and the American dream that tells us that if you just work for what you want, you will succeed, so if you're not succeeding in life, it is because you have not tried hard enough. A constant drip-feed of this attitude over decades has led to the point where it's now become acceptable to denigrate both the working class and the poor, particularly those on benefits. We can so easily start to see poverty as a personal failing. While it is true that some people face poverty due to bad decisions they have made, most of us are only two or three bad choices or circumstances beyond our control away from a crisis that could so easily entrap us in a downward spiral. And the reality is that 66 percent of people in poverty in Britain today live in households where at least one person works.[44] In fact, as mentioned earlier, in 2016 a new term was coined—'JAMs'—to describe a group of about six million households who are 'just about managing' to make ends meet: they are in work, but are struggling to get by, and typically have less than a month's income in savings.[45]

If we are going to build churches where the poor or the working class can find community in the same way as the middle class or any other group, we need to keep a close watch on our attitudes towards those in need. It is incredibly easy for us to move from 'being disgusted by poverty' to being 'disgusted by poor people themselves', as Suzanne Moore puts it in *The Guardian*.[46] This is especially the case if we have started to confuse which of our values are biblical and which are just middle class. We can become so familiar with things being done a certain way that we can fail to realise that it is just our custom or habit or tradition, and not necessarily the 'right' way of doing things.

We mentioned earlier that we need to be intentionally thoughtful if we're to build a church for all. This hit home for me (Natalie) on an Alpha course in my church, where a man who had been attending decided he wanted to become a Christian. I had the privilege, along with another member of the team, of leading him in a prayer and praying for him. When we'd finished, the other team member started to explain to the man the importance of reading his Bible. I knew that the man couldn't read, so I quickly interjected that audio versions are available. But it highlighted to me just how easily we can make assumptions, and how much effort it takes for us to try to be aware of potential differences that may exist.

Relationships are key. If we surround ourselves with people 'just like us', then we will find it difficult to understand the way other people think. We'll also miss out on the opportunity to express the beauty of the gospel that crosses all dividing walls and unites us as the people of God. We are citizens of heaven, not of this neighbourhood or that neighbourhood, this tribe or that tribe, this nation or that nation. Proximity to poverty softens our hearts towards people who have less than us. It gives us real, live opportunities for increasing compassion, kindness and generosity.

But it's all too easy to slip into pushing for behaviour modification. When we follow Jesus, we are changed by him. That's true. But if we are not careful we can try to convert people to middle class ways of living more than a renewing of their minds to the ways of life in Christ. For example, we might expect them to start inviting people to their house for dinner, rather than expressing the biblical value of hospitality in a way that might come more naturally to them—perhaps having an open house where people drop in unannounced at any time during the day, or having people to stay. (In fact, some of these expressions of hospitality might be more radical in our culture than inviting someone for a nice middle class dinner party!)

If I pay attention to my own heart, I find that the more time I spend with people facing poverty, the more aware I am of *my* need to change, more than theirs. Part of this comes from being very aware of my own tendency to want to reach down to help people, rather than to consider them equals from whom I have as much to learn, if not more. Part of a middle class mentality can be wanting to 'do good' at arm's length. However, if we truly believe that each one of us is made in the image of God, then we need to be immersed in each other's lives, even when we're uncomfortable, so that we can see God reflected in the other person and learn more about him through them. If the poor or working class are uncomfortable in our churches, we don't need to convert them to our middle class ways. We need to move out of our comfort zones and accept them as they are. As Darren Edwards says, allowing people to be both Christians *and* working class is a biblical mandate: 'Each person should remain in the situation they were in when God called them' (1 Cor. 7:20).

When people don't come to us—as the working class aren't coming to our churches—we need to find ways to reach out. But we cannot do it with an attitude of superiority. We simply must not approach wanting to draw working class and poorer people into our churches as something we 'do to them'. If we're to see churches that truly reflect all classes and economic situations, we need to be prepared to move into neighbourhoods that have bad reputations, to place our children in schools that may not achieve the best results, to shop where shopkeepers get to know their customers, to listen to people who we may feel we cannot relate to at all.

Proximity to poverty doesn't necessarily enable us to build churches where those from different backgrounds can integrate with one another and find family across class and other boundaries. There are scores of people pioneering church plants on council estates across the country. This is a good thing, but we must be careful to build churches where everyone is welcome; where those 'not like us' (whether we're middle class, working class, facing poverty or wealthy) feel at home too. The church that Jesus died for is gloriously diverse in every way—it is 'the manifold wisdom of God' (Eph. 3:10) and is at its most beautiful and powerful when it demonstrates the unity and reconciliation that comes through Jesus. One of the most exciting baptism celebrations I've been to was one where a police officer and a former prisoner stood side-by-side, about to be baptised one after the other, with the guy who had previously committed crime after crime able to say that the man who used to arrest him was now his brother in Christ. It displays the full glory of the gospel when those who would never have mixed in human terms can stand shoulder-to-shoulder because of what Jesus has done in their lives. This is true across enemy lines, ethnic divisions, and class boundaries. Wherever there is division, the church is to demonstrate reconciliation. So we need churches where the working class and the middle class sit together, speak with one another, share food and faith and find community that transcends postcodes and income levels and educational achievements.

Paul Brown has been reaching out to working class communities in London for twenty years and is one of the leaders at City Hope Church in London. He has also researched class issues affecting churches in Britain. In his unpublished paper 'Silence in Class', he writes: 'You may think you've won a nation when you've influenced the arts, the media, the banking systems, the movers and shakers of the nation but until you've impacted the white working classes no amount of success elsewhere will compensate the church for failure here.'

If we are to build churches for all, we need to break out of mindsets that may have been formed by our own background and class or by the media and political narratives that surround us. Some of the ways we do this are:

Seeing God as he is

When we spend time seeking God's heart, through prayer, Bible reading and corporate worship in particular, we are increasingly sanctified—made more like Jesus. It doesn't happen by osmosis, but by deliberate submission to God and alignment with his ways. When we start intentionally pursuing God's heart for the poor, and for people in general, we find ourselves with more opportunities to grow in generosity and compassion. This is the antidote to any cultural prejudices we may have picked up along the way, but we have to be active and not passive.

Seeing ourselves as we are

We need to have a sober assessment of ourselves, asking God to highlight any biases we have and any commitment to middle class values that is unhelpful to reaching others who may not share them. I am trying to learn to let my first question, when I feel uncomfortable or judgmental or fearful around someone, be 'what is going on in my heart?' before I start to ask questions about the person in front of me. I find that so often bad attitudes lurk just below the surface, masquerading as gospel imperatives when in fact they are just the way I am used to doing things. At the same time, we need to recognise our calling as God's people—co-labourers with Christ, his ambassadors, ministers of reconciliation. As such, we can expect God to use us and equip us to transcend barriers of culture or class or material wealth.

Seeing others as they are

It is crucial that we recognise that everyone is made in the image of God and has been uniquely designed to reflect him to others. This image of God is still present in all people despite the destructive power of sin. This is the paradox we face. We are often shaped in our view of people by their sinfulness and mistakes and inadequacies. However, we should also remember that they still bear the image of God and have the capacity, through the redeeming power of Christ, to reflect something of that image to others. We can inadvertently limit God and the people we encounter by having too small a view of the gospel's power. God's vision for people isn't that they modify their behaviour and become nice, polite middle class Christians. It is that they become 'oaks of righteousness'— leaders in their communities and churches—rebuilders, restorers, renewers of places that have been devastated for generations (Isa. 61:3-4). God's heart for those in need isn't simply that they should be given handouts to paper over the cracks, but that they should be completely transformed. I visited a church in London not long ago, where a friend pointed out to me the worship leader, explaining that he'd come to the night shelter two years ago when he was homeless. He had found help for his immediate needs of a safe and dry place to sleep and food to eat. He had found friendship too, and then he found active faith in Jesus. Within two years, he had secured accommodation, become part of the worship team in the church, got married, had a son and then, just recently, taken a homeless person into his house. All this had happened without him changing from one class to another, and without any expectation on him from the church to adapt to a particular class culture. He was embraced as he was. The changes in his life have been based on his commitment to following Jesus, rather than conforming to be like others in the congregation. These stories may seem few and far between, but they are what the gospel is all about. This is God's vision for those in poverty.

Seeing what changes we need to make

As we have already said, if we are to see churches where rich and poor, middle class and working class, black and white, are all family together, there will be some changes we need to make. We need to become more aware of how our practices might be off-putting to people from different backgrounds. We need to resist the temptation to leap in with quick fixes, instead committing ourselves for the long-haul. The church leader who pointed out to me that my church has 'held onto' people from a working class or poor background, also explained that there are no hard and fast solutions. All of us come to Jesus with messy, broken backgrounds in one way or another. Sometimes it's just more hidden and less obvious. God works in us slowly. We are often less patient! We want to see outward change quickly. But building churches where people from all different backgrounds form community is a time-consuming, painstaking, decades-long process. We need to be committed to it, and committed to the people God puts in our path.

PART TWO:
A CHURCH FOR THE POOR—THE PRACTICALITIES

EIGHT

BUILDING A CHURCH FOR THE POOR—CALLING

The history of the church in Britain tells us an interesting thing—when God moves in revival power it almost always starts with the poor and ordinary working people. Think of the Quaker movement of the seventeenth century. It was a working class revival based on George Fox's dynamic preaching tours and informal 'heart on your sleeves' worship, which scandalised the establishment of the day. Think of the eighteenth century Methodist movement we discussed earlier. Wesley and Whitefield aimed to reach the common man from the beginning with outdoor preaching to the masses, a mid-week group system suited to the uneducated, and a culture of social inclusion across the classes. Think again of the early twentieth century Welsh Revival, which had such a profound impact on the working classes of Wales. In the early days the chapels were filled with shopworkers, farm labourers and miners.

But here's the flip side. Over time, spiritually renewed churches always seem to become 'gentrified' until they become dominated numerically and culturally by the middle classes. There are various reasons for this tendency to 'gentrification'. One cause is often the lack of radical church leadership to keep challenging the church not to settle for a comfortable lifestyle, but to be engaged in radical mission and discipleship. Another factor is that committed Christians tended to work hard and improve their living standards over time. This process can accidentally lead to 'gentrification' over time. This happened to the Quakers, who within a hundred years of George Fox's ministry had become an intellectual branch of middle class Nonconformity. What about the mighty Methodist movement? During the nineteenth century it gradually became middle class in both leadership and membership. What about the churches that were touched by the Welsh Revival? Their spiritual life began to drain away from the 1920s onwards—and the working classes began to drift away at the same time.

Let's fast forward this discussion and take a look at the UK church today. With a few notable exceptions, the British church is a middle class affair. Let's start with social geography. Just ask yourself this question: where are the bigger and better resourced churches in your area? On the working class estates and deprived inner-city areas? Or in the more affluent suburban or city centre locations? I think I can guess the answer! And your answer is likely to be the same as mine and that of most readers. Now let's think about leadership. What is the social profile of church leaders in your area? Are they generally from middle class backgrounds with a good education? I think I can guess your answer again!

Now there is nothing intrinsically wrong with having strong churches in middle class areas led by mostly middle class leaders. Those churches still have a vital mission in those areas, which is to be strongly endorsed. Some people are called to that type of mission specifically and this is a good thing—all people need reaching for Christ. After all, middle class people can suffer from 'relational poverty' as much as anyone else. However, the social geography of the church in Britain must surely make us uncomfortable and provoke us to ask a few searching questions about the generally unreached working classes, which include many in poverty and severe social need. It is shocking to observe how far removed by distance, culture and relationship the poor usually are from churches in their area. Now if this is true for the long-established white and black working classes and poor—then what about those coming into Britain? The UK is currently experiencing a significant wave of immigration. Tens of thousands of Eastern Europeans, Africans, Arabs and others are seeking to settle here and work in our country.[47] Many coming from outside Europe are asylum seekers, fleeing from dreadful situations in their own nations. Many are poor. Many are needy. How are our largely middle class churches going to reach these new residents in our country? And what about those on benefits, who might feel marginalised by their portrayal in the media and stigmatised even by some in our churches as those who are just after something for nothing?

There is a great risk before us at this point. The case I (Martin) have made is hard to refute in terms of the facts on the ground. Yet it can induce guilt rather than positive conviction. Guilt will lead us down a slippery slope—and the slope involves churches and individuals making knee-jerk responses to social needs around them. We can sometimes be motivated by the media, by an articulate and disgruntled church member, by some dramatic local situation or by a persuasive community leader who knocks on the door of the church asking for help. However, knee-jerk reactions to social need can be a risky starting point and usually lead to difficulties. Such responses can sometimes lead to fruitful and effective care for the poor, but only when we've given thought to ensuring they are not just short-term, boom and bust projects that cannot be sustained.

Let me suggest an alternative approach. In my experience working with churches across the country, I have noticed four factors that have a decisive and positive impact on local churches in moving them forward in social engagement and seeking to create a church for the poor.

Biblical conviction

We have already seen how the early church prioritised caring for the poor. However, we now need to look a bit more closely at what the membership of the actual church communities looked like in those early days.

Jesus always intended his church to be populated significantly by the poor and marginalised (see Luke 4:14-21). Many of us are so used to sitting in comfortable churches alongside mostly well-off people that we can think this is normal. It is not. Norms are set by Scripture, not by our experience. Jesus was unequivocal about his primary mission. He came to 'proclaim good news to the poor' (Luke 4:18). This is not a poetic expression—it became a literal reality in Jesus' ministry. Tens of thousands of needy people came to meet him. He brought to them miraculous power to meet their immediate needs and he also offered them spiritual transformation through the message of the good news. They could be forgiven their sins and granted new life. The implication of this is clear— these ordinary and often impoverished people were offered the possibility of becoming part of the church that was to come into being after Jesus' resurrection. There was to be no special place at the table for the elites of the day—they were very welcome in churches, but they came but as equals who could offer to use their wealth and their social advantages to serve others.

In case we think for a moment that this was just an idealistic pipe dream of Jesus', let's read how Paul describes the churches he was establishing across the Roman world:

> Brothers and sisters, think of what you were when you were called. Not many of you were wise by human standards; not many were influential; not many were of noble birth. But God chose the foolish things of the world to shame the wise; God chose the weak things of the world to shame the strong. God chose the lowly things of this world and the despised things—and the things that are not—to nullify the things that are, so that no one may boast before him. (1 Cor. 1:26-29)

And it wasn't just Paul who thought like this. Here is James:

> Has not God chosen those who are poor in the eyes of the world to be rich in faith and to inherit

the kingdom he promised those who love him?
(James 2:5)

We are left with the unmistakable impression that the churches of
the apostolic period were not middle class enclaves, but a wonderful
social mix of classes and races and cultures with a strong numerical
representation within them of people who were relatively or absolutely poor. This was indeed a church for the poor.

Personal experience

We are all shaped by our personal experience. I described in chapter
one how my time spent living and working in South Africa had a
formative effect on who I am and how I think. People come to
faith in Christ with many complex and painful experiences behind
them. There can be trauma, loss, sickness, bereavement and much
more. There can be positive experiences too, of course. They are all
formative. They all need processing and reflection in the light of
faith in Christ.

This may seem like simply stating the obvious. But there is
another thing about personal experience that I have observed that
is far less obvious, but is very important.

The Holy Spirit often uses our personal experience to form part
of our sense of calling to serve the poor or marginalised. This was
certainly the case in Natalie's story as described in chapter one. I
wonder if you can recognise that process in yourself or in your
Christian friends? It is good to think this through and recognise
what is happening. My own view is that this is generally a very

positive factor in the development of mercy ministries in the church.

Here is an example. In my church we have for many years run a special after school club for children from the community. Some years ago, one of the children who attended this club was killed near his home in a tragic road accident. This death had a huge impact on the workers in the children's club—as would be expected. One issue that arose was how to help the young boy's surviving siblings cope with the loss of their brother. This experience led, over a period of time, to the development of a specialist ministry of the church aimed at supporting school children who had been bereaved in their families. That project is now well established and works mostly through local schools. Humanly speaking, this project would never have come into being without the very painful personal experiences surrounding the earlier tragic death of a young boy on the road.

Community circumstances

The focus of any church must be rooted in its locality. Every area is different and has differing demographics, economic factors, types of need and patterns of poverty. One thing I noticed when I started out as a church pastor many years ago was how many elderly people lived in the district near the church. This was a favoured part of town for people to move to in retirement. My wife and I were involved in relating to the elderly in our area for some time and noticed the level of loneliness and vulnerability behind many a well presented front door. So we started up a social club for the elderly.

We have long since handed this over to others, but it has now been an active ministry of the church for many years—and hundreds have been impacted and supported. Some have come to faith along the way.

It is important for churches to look closely at their communities. Some needs will be obvious. Others are below the surface, but still very real. Talking to local councillors helps. They know more than most people what is really going on locally. Sometimes we are able to reach out to the most vulnerable only after some research and reflection has identified a particular group in need.

Then there are the general national trends that can stimulate the church into action. We saw a dramatic example of this after the financial crash of 2008. This was a huge economic shock for our nation. Serious consequences soon followed: rapid changes to the benefits system, cuts in local government services and a fresh wave of unemployment led to the emergence of serious levels of need. The small pre-existing foodbank movement suddenly multiplied across the country as churches responded to the urgent need for emergency intervention.

At about the same time, the Street Pastors movement developed in a similar way. The impetus came from the black majority churches across Britain as they sought to respond to the serious threat of gun and knife crime rooted in the gang culture of our inner cities. Hundreds of churches have followed the lead of the black majority churches and have taken up the cause. Street Pastors has become a national movement almost overnight and is a resource to deal with much more than gun and knife crime. Other similar initiatives have also developed.[48]

And now our country faces a much more serious challenge in terms of immigration, the arrival of refugees and the asylum-seeking process. The numbers are growing and are likely to continue to do so. Housing shortage is at a critical level. The needs of refugees are often urgent. The church is slowly rising to the challenge. The story of how we respond to the rising tide of refugees will be told over the next decade or two. It is yet to be written.

Prophetic leading

Not every church can respond fully to every need. Focus is vital. Some of that focus comes through knowing your area and its key issues. However, there is another dimension—the prophetic. We live in an age that is rediscovering the prophetic dimension of being church. The Holy Spirit speaks to particular churches and individuals about particular opportunities and callings. It was like this in the days of the early church. Just imagine yourself as a member of the newly formed and fast growing church in Antioch (Acts 11:19-30). We mentioned this church in chapter three, but the story is worth considering again in this context. Antioch was the first major cosmopolitan cross-cultural church. It had great leaders, good teaching, a constant flow of new people coming to join. It was a growing and dynamic church. Then one day the leaders introduced a special visitor from Jerusalem. His name was Agabus and he was known as a prophet. Agabus stood before the church and made a surprising prediction—a famine was going to take place soon that would have serious consequences, especially in the most economically vulnerable regions. The church considered this prophetic prediction and concluded it was authentic and needed a response. They then decided that their sister churches in and around Jerusalem were likely to suffer most in a future famine and so they asked the congregation to give money so that they could send a substantial gift to the church in Jerusalem to be used when the predicted famine struck (Acts 11:27-30). It is a remarkable story, but what is even more remarkable is that such a famine did indeed take place! There is a lot we don't know about this story, but what we do know indicates the power of prophecy to shape a church's engagement with the poor.

Let me illustrate this from my own experience as a church leader. I took over leading Barnabas Community Church, Shrews-bury, in 1994. I subsequently led the church for twenty years. We soon purchased an old army drill hall in the town centre for the church to use. It became something of a community centre and the base for our social action projects. During those early days I often reflected on the fact that all the bigger churches in our town were based in the centre or the southern suburbs, which were the richer parts of town. The north of town had some big working class estates that had hardly any church presence at all. Then one day, while at a prayer and fasting retreat for church leaders, I sensed the words come into my mind: 'Plant a church in Harlescott.' I imme-diately knew what this meant. Harlescott was one of those northern districts with poorer estates. Many people on those estates would never consider connecting with a church in the centre or south of the town—the cultural and economic gap was too big. So, to cut a long story short, after much consideration our leadership team and church members embraced the vision to plant a new church.

Then we identified a leader and a core team of 'church planters' and worked towards this surprising and unlikely goal. It took four years to move from the idea to the reality of a small congregation gathered and meeting in the north of town. There were many challenges along the way. We made some mistakes in how we went about things. However, over ten years later the church is now well established and thriving, with many members from the local estates. What is more, we have maintained a close relationship between the two 'sister' churches. We help each other in our joint mission to reach different parts of our town.

The point of this story is simple—to illustrate the creative role of prophetic words in leading us towards building a church for the poor. There are many ways to go about achieving this goal. Church planting is just one of them.

Conclusion

So here are four key factors that usually have a place in the process of being called to work to build a church for the poor: biblical conviction, personal experience, community circumstances and prophetic leading. All of them will help us on the journey.

NINE

BUILDING A CHURCH FOR THE POOR—CULTURE

As soon as we start thinking about extending the mission of a local church we start to face a big issue—culture. If we are trying to attract different social groups to the church community we have to start thinking about the culture they come from and the main culture of the church. There is often a big gap between the two. This is a common problem in the outreach of the church. Will black people be willing to come to a white-majority church (and vice versa)? How can the church attract teenagers when the average age of the congregation might be over 50? How does the church reach out to new groups of Eastern European immigrants in its neighbourhood?

These are vital questions for churches to contemplate.

However, the question of culture often becomes even more difficult when we consider building a church for the poor. A whole range of complex questions come flooding into our minds: How do recovering addicts relate to the wider church community? What would we do to welcome incoming refugees into our churches? How do we connect foodbank clients to the church community? What about people who don't learn easily through conceptual teaching? What about those who have lost all confidence in socialising?

You will probably be familiar with these and many similar questions.

Before trying to address the question of cultural issues we face, let's step back for a moment to think about what the church is intended to be according to the Bible. When we look closely at the New Testament we find a startling reality—the church was the most radical social institution of the day! The gospel of Christ gave everyone an equal starting point when they entered the church. Good social background did not give any privileges—all were brothers and sisters (James 2:1-4). Also, very strikingly, the great social divides of the day were overcome in the church. Paul makes clear that 'there is neither Jew nor Gentile, neither slave nor free, nor is there male and female, for you are all one in Christ Jesus' (Gal. 3:28). Paul was talking about the largest social divides of the Roman Empire—divides that generally kept people apart. It was to be the opposite in the church. The Jews had to relinquish their sense of spiritual and racial superiority arising from their understanding of their special status in the Old Testament. Slaves were not to be treated differently because of their lack of freedom and wealth. Women were not to be treated as second class citizens on the grounds of their gender. This whole process was all about cultures meeting and taking their place alongside each other in the church community.

However, this is not the end of the story. Paul went even further—he called the church to hold its prevailing culture very lightly as it reached out to those of different cultures. Paul described his own attempt to do this in 1 Corinthians 9:19-23:

> Though I am free and belong to no one, I have made myself a slave to everyone, to win as many as possible. To the Jews I became like a Jew, to win the Jews. To those under the law I became like one under the law (though I myself am not under the law), so as to win those under the law. To those not having the law I became like one not having the law (though I am not free from God's law but am under Christ's law), so as to win those not having the law. To the weak I became weak, to win the weak. I have become all things to all people so that by all possible means I might save some. I do all this for the sake of the gospel, that I may share in its blessings.

Paul was in no doubt that he had to cross cultural barriers in order to advance the gospel and communicate effectively with those in other cultures. The central challenge for Paul was to bridge the huge cultural gap between the Jews and other nationalities of the Roman Empire. That wasn't an easy thing to do because the Jews had so many rules and regulations that marked them out as different from everyone else!

What we can conclude from this quick look at the New Testament is that the church is designed to be a multicultural community where there is space for all sorts of people to belong and flourish. Let's now take a close look at the reality on the ground that most of us will be familiar with in churches we know or belong to. We know it doesn't always look quite like the New Testament picture!

If you go into any church meeting on a Sunday you can quickly work out some key features of its culture. You can look at the age profile or the racial composition. You can get an idea about the general educational level. You can see if there are university students there. You can see the style of leadership. You can notice if more than one language is spoken, and so on. There are many subtle signs of culture that an observant person can quickly notice when they walk into a meeting.

However, what you are seeing is what I like to call the 'main culture' of the church. Behind that main culture are various subcultures. Let's take a simple example. Imagine you visit a church for the first time and notice a large group of teenagers in the meeting. They are all sitting together, they dress a little differently to the rest of the people, they tend to be on their mobile phones through the meeting and they tend to socialise with each other and maybe a handful of other adults at the end. To be honest, they don't look hugely excited during the meeting—but they are there, and seem reasonably comfortable to be there. One of their group is in the worship band and one of their current favourite songs is used during the time of worship. There is a noticeable increase in engagement during that particular song. Also, the youth leader sits at the front with the other pastors of the church. However, if you had the chance to go to their mid-week youth meeting you would find that the music is louder, the talk is shorter, the lights are lower and the atmosphere is cooler!

So what's going on here? It's a classic case of the relationship between the main culture and a particular sub-culture in a church. It is a subtle relationship—and not often considered carefully enough. What tends to make a church function well as a community is an effective link between the main culture and the various sub-cultures represented there. So, let's return to our example of the teenagers for a moment. They are obviously most at home in their own sub-culture in their mid-week youth meeting. However, they come on Sunday largely because their sub-culture is represented to some extent by what happens: a member of their group is in the worship band, their leader is publicly recognised at the front of the church and some of their music tastes are represented in the worship.

Now, let's turn this example on its head. Imagine that in this church that I have described to you there is a change of leadership. The new senior pastor makes some changes: he makes a new rule that only over 18s can play in the worship band, he suggests to the youth leader that his place on Sunday is sitting with his family, not at the front. Also he changes the song list for Sunday mornings to remove any songs that he feels are trivial and introspective—such as the song I just mentioned. It has to be said that the new pastor is also under pressure from some of the senior members of the church who feel that Sundays have become too casual and informal.

Let's just analyse this simple story for a minute. It is all about the link between the main and sub-cultures within a church—they can be strong links or very weak links. This depends on how the culture is set by the leaders. From a New Testament point of view, it appears that it is an important skill of leaders to set the main culture so that all the significant sub-cultures in the church feel that they have a stake in the main culture. They need to be represented there as well as having a place where they can flourish in a sub-cultural context: social events, personal friendships, mid-week home groups, social media groups and the like. A mature church has a number of flourishing sub-cultures whose members feel both a security in their own sub-culture and an ownership of the main church culture, which, of course, takes them somewhat out of their sub-cultural comfort zone.

The goal, of course, is that gradually all the sub-cultures will become so much a part of the main culture, that they become indistinguishable and inseparable from each other. How will we know when this has happened? When people from the sub-cultures fully and spontaneously participate in the full breadth of church activities. During the writing of this book, Natalie received an email from a friend telling her the following story:

> We had a homeless guy—a dear friend now after four years, though not yet saved—pray out loud through the microphone tonight for the first time when we lifted our plans to work with the housing charity Green Pastures. He prayed: 'God, if you're real, and you're the God of the impossible, then I'm the impossible. I'll become a Christian if you make this happen this year. Now let us pray, we'll

pray—the church.' The response was phenome-
nal—we love this guy and though he's not saved
and not a member we really want him to feel at
home enough to hear the gospel (through worship,
preaching, friendship, loving challenge, etc.) and
we're learning to love people as they are, trusting
Jesus to effect change!

Let's put it another way. The church is like a human body, according
to Paul in 1 Corinthians 12. God's plan is that in that 'body' people
of very different characteristics and abilities can contribute and all
pull together to make the church work well and represent the
universal character of the gospel. This is often described as 'unity
in diversity'. The unity factor is based on our common faith in
Christ and our common commitment to a particular church. The
diversity factor is the amazing range of age, personality, skills and
cultures represented in any healthy church community. This week,
as I write this chapter, I have had the joy of publicly welcoming,
on Sunday, the (currently) youngest person in our church
community who is a few days old, while also visiting our oldest
member, aged 95, who is recovering in a convalescent home from
an accident.

Let's illustrate this question of church culture more specifically
by taking an example. The church I have in mind was planted
intentionally in a poorer, working class area. It has a small but
flourishing congregation and has seen some real success in terms of
reaching out to the local community. For example, shortly before
I wrote this section there was a joyful service in the church in

which a number of young people from the area were baptised and told their stories of coming to faith. The church leaders have consciously adopted a number of strategies to address the question of culture. Firstly, the leaders themselves have decided to live in the heart of the community and have all moved house to enable this to happen. Their children attend the nearest schools and the leaders seek to be engaged with local community life as much as possible. This sends a key cultural signal to those who might think of joining their church.

Secondly, the Alpha course as an evangelistic resource has been adapted in small but significant ways. Many people in the community are not comfortable with going out in the evening to an Alpha event in which they are also expected to participate in group discussion. Neither formal evening meetings nor group discussion are part of their experience. So the church has often used the Alpha course material in a one-to-one context rather than in an evening meeting structure. These one-to-one contexts also enable those with reading or learning difficulties to feel more secure as they explore the truths of the Christian faith.

Thirdly, the conduct of Sunday morning church meetings is particularly informal and welcoming to newcomers and those not familiar with public church meetings. Also, those who have joined the church from the local area are given responsibility in Sunday church life as soon as possible and so they become contributors to the cultural life of the church.

Fourthly, church social events reflect local community culture. For example, they run regular Bingo Nights in their church hall. These are now well established, popular and enabling the church to build bridges into the community. Another telling example concerns coffee! The current popularity of high quality coffee in churches has not influenced this church. Instant coffee is the order of the day both in terms of local community culture and the church budget!

This brings us to the important question of finance. Many church members are relatively poor. Generous giving is encouraged, but the sums given by many members are modest. As a result, money is not invested in the ways in which many more wealthy churches might take for granted. So, for example, the PA equipment is simple and the IT budget is small.

Another example worth exploring here is what it might look like to make our churches more racially inclusive. Earlier we looked at the importance of not just talking about diversity, but ensuring we are inclusive in practice by not just having white, middle class, married people (for example) on the platform or in the pulpit. There is, of course, a danger that our desire to create more diversity leads to tokenism. We might invite someone with a different skin colour to join our worship team, for example, as a deliberate move to ensure that all of our public personalities are not white. But where this happens regardless of talent or ability, it will easily be spotted as a token gesture, with people who aren't white realising what has happened and people who are white possibly being upset that they cannot get into the worship band even though they're more talented than those in it.

The answer to this is to seriously invest in people. If you want more people who are black or Asian or poor or female in leadership roles, spend time with them, get to know them, give them opportunities in smaller settings, such as small groups and prayer meetings, then provide honest feedback to help them grow into leaders who can hold their own. Ben, who leads a congregation in London, says:

> You can preach a heart for this stuff, but you have to then pursue it. We are to be diverse not because it's a bug-bear but because it's a biblical mandate. It is really important to understand that Jesus died for all, not just for one particular culture. This is clear in Acts 1:8 and Acts 10:34-35, for example. We should never be satisfied when our churches are just one culture or homogenous because that doesn't reflect the fact that Jesus died for everyone. So leadership needs to be inclusive, welcoming, understanding what's going on locally, opening their homes up to different people. Humble yourself and appreciate your way isn't necessarily right and the norm for you isn't the norm for others.

One step all of us can take—whether in leadership or not—is walking across the room to build relationships. Diversity is not the end goal. Building a New Testament church that reflects Jesus is the reason diversity is important. Some of us are in diverse churches but never mix with those in the congregation who are from different backgrounds. A teenager who recently moved from a London borough to my (Natalie's) church said he noticed immediately that black people sit in one section on Sundays—it was so stark to him that he asked if we had set aside that area specifically! This reflects a challenge to our churches to be places where diversity means integration of different types of people. If people from a working class background, or who are single, or who are elderly, all sit together and do not have meaningful relationships with people 'not like them', we have stopped short of building New Testament churches. Discussing this with a friend recently, she said: 'Why do we have to move, though? Why is it our responsibility rather than theirs?' Any of us in the majority can be prone to think like this, but because we are in the majority, the onus is on us. As Ben puts it: 'Any church I've seen flourish like this is where those in the majority culture break their backs to make people welcome.'

There simply is no substitute for listening to someone's own account of their experiences and background. Whenever I hear people expressing resentment to Eastern Europeans who move over to the UK for work, I wonder if they've ever heard a Romanian or Bulgarian talk about their struggle to support their children while earning the equivalent of maybe two pounds a day as a skilled professional in their country. When I have heard stories such as this directly, something changes in my heart so that my question is no longer: 'Why have you come here?' but is instead: 'Why wouldn't you come here?' If we really want to understand people from other countries and cultures, so that we can truly understand what inadvertent barriers our churches might be putting up for an affluent black professional or a poverty stricken white person or a pregnant white teenage girl or a black teenager at risk of dropping out of school, we need to get to know people.

Some aspects of the culture of our church life are more obvious than others. If we live in an area with a diverse population, yet our church members are all people with similar backgrounds, this is clearly noticeable. But many elements of the culture we have set in our churches are not. For example, if your small group meetings are mainly organised in a WhatsApp group or your serving rotas are accessed through an app, it might make it difficult for people who don't own a smartphone or who struggle with literacy to feel they can participate. Likewise, if it's common for people in your group to bring expensive bottles of drink to social gatherings, someone with less disposable income may feel pressure to try to fit in, or they may feel excluded from the group as a result of not being able to afford the same as everyone else.

The church in the UK is currently addressing this issue of culture more directly and with more energy than at any time in the recent past. There are a number of reasons for this trend that are worth noting here. Firstly, the recent rise in church-based social action, which we documented in our first book,[49] has led the church to reconsider mission to the poorest and most marginalised. Secondly, there has been a clear lead in this direction given by senior church leaders such as the Archbishop of Canterbury, Justin Welby.[50] Thirdly, the Catholic Church has engaged afresh with issues of poverty since the appointment of Pope Francis (see chapter ten). Fourthly, there has been a heightened awareness in recent years of the surprisingly high levels of poverty in the UK. Finally, it is worth noting the increasing awareness in the UK of the marginalisation and disenfranchisement of the working class estates across the country. Many factors have been involved in this sense of alienation and disenfranchisement: long-term unemployment, mass immigration from the EU, welfare reforms, and the rise of the narrative of the 'undeserving poor' in the media. This reality came dramatically to the forefront of UK national life during the EU referendum of 2016 in which the success of the 'Leave' campaign was, in part, attributed by observers to strong support from traditional working class groups who felt disenfranchised from the political process and the elite culture of decision-makers in the UK. Those same working class groups are among those who are most disconnected from the church.

All this has focused the thinking and the energy of the churches in a fresh way. The task of building a church for the poor seems increasingly urgent. But it's not easy. Many Christians, including church leaders, are asking the question: 'How do we take care of the poor from being like a department of church life to being in the heart of who we are as a people?' It's a challenging question. It requires us to look at what we do well now—perhaps we are helping more people than we did five years ago; perhaps we mention those in need in our sermons more often—and to look at what we want to do well in the future. Maybe in ten years' time we would like to have brought people through from one of our social action projects to leadership roles in the church. Maybe we want to see our spending on care for the poor increase until it is at least ten percent of our annual expenditure. Comparing where we are now to where we want to be a few years down the line is the first step in working out the strategy to change the culture.

There are also many questions for us to ask ourselves individually. If we want to belong to churches where people of all classes and financial situations can feel at home, we need to be cultivating certain attitudes in our lives. Are we growing in kindness? Are we looking for opportunities to be generous? Are we more concerned about looking like 'good Christians' or actually becoming like Jesus? Are we more preoccupied with how we can bless, serve and give or how we can be blessed, benefit from church life and receive? What do our lifestyles—our social activities, our bank balances, the people we spend our time with—say about what is really important to us?

Changing the culture of our churches might also mean taking a cold, sober look at the prejudices in our hearts. Do we genuinely believe working in McDonald's is as worthwhile as working in an office or for the church, for example? Do we genuinely believe that a homeless drug addict can reflect something of the image of God powerfully to us just as a lead elder can? Do we believe our value comes from being made in the image of God, or have we bought into the lie that it comes from status, position and/or wealth? Do we really believe the gospel has the power to transform lives, or have we let what we've seen (or haven't) dictate what we expect? Are we only interested in helping those who are grateful and making adjustments to their behaviour that mean they're becoming 'more like us'?

To truly establish a church for the poor will affect us individually, because each Christian is called to radical discipleship, and following after Jesus requires us to be increasingly loving, kind, merciful, generous, forgiving and compassionate. But it will also affect every area of church life—preaching, small groups, youth, worship, leadership teams, budgets, children's work and more. For this we need strategy.

TEN

BUILDING A CHURCH FOR THE POOR—STRATEGY

As we stated in the last chapter, there has been a huge rise in church engagement with the poor in recent years in the UK. The story is well-known and has been thoroughly documented.[51] For many churches this increase in social action is the whole story of their engagement with the poor. Such churches are happy to state what they are doing for those in need in their area. They are glad to describe this in terms of 'human flourishing' or 'community transformation'. For many this is what is meant by being a church for the poor—the resources and energies of the church are being given over sacrificially to help those in need.

This is all good and commendable. But it is not exactly what we mean in this book by the expression 'a church for the poor'. Social action is only a part of the story. If we stop there, then we run the big risk that, for the most part, churches will still be relationally and culturally disconnected from the people they are helping. Sometimes social action projects accidentally reinforce existing social divides.

What about the evangelistic responsibility of the church towards the poor? What about enabling the poor to become a full part of the community of the church? What about discipling new believers from poor backgrounds? These are tough questions that require robust answers.

The UK church is very diverse. There are significant differences in the approaches taken to this issue as one might expect. Most readers, if they are churchgoers, will come from within a particular tradition. Well, now we are going to look beyond our own experiences. We are going to take time to have a brief look at the significant and very diverse initiatives in the UK church as it seeks to address the challenge to be a church for the poor.

Parishes and charities—a Catholic perspective

The Roman Catholic Church has considered this issue of a church for the poor carefully in recent years. The stimulus for this has come right from the top. As I (Martin) write this chapter Pope Francis has just celebrated his eightieth birthday—by having a meal with some homeless people! His papacy has been full of symbolic acts of this sort which send a very clear message to Catholics around the world. From the outset of his papacy Pope Francis memorably called the Catholic Church to be 'a poor church for the poor'.[52]

There is a long and distinguished history of Catholic lay social activism in the UK as represented by the thousands of volunteers of the Vincent de Paul Society[53] and the supporters of movements such as Focolare,[54] the Young Christian Workers movement[55] and the Justice and Peace Network.[56] Also, at a theological level there has been a recent revival of interest in Catholic Social Teaching (CST).[57] This has been strongly endorsed by Pope Francis. The Catholic Church as an institution reaches out to the poor in the UK mostly through the work of Catholic charities whose efforts are facilitated by support from local parishes. This process is enabled, in part, by the national Caritas Social Action Network (CSAN).[58] This approach has meant that Catholics have not generally been the driving force behind the recent rise in church-based social action projects. The community franchise model[59] that underpins much of this trend is not central to the focus of many Catholic clergy who tend to work mostly through their own local initiatives or through well established Catholic charities.

My Catholic friends often acknowledge that a truly holistic and evangelistic mission to the poor is a big challenge to their church in the UK. The focus of their social action initiatives tends to be based on the CST doctrine of 'solidarity' with little emphasis on a more direct evangelistic approach or on the implications of full integration of the poor into parish communities as renewed or newly believing Christians. CSAN sees two of its key objectives as bringing 'compassion and heartfelt care, as exemplified by the life of Jesus' to those in need and ensuring 'justice and respect for human dignity and life'.[60]

Having said all this, the outworking of Catholic social activism is very varied across the country and in many places the Catholic Church at the parish level is still focused mostly on strengthening its existing congregations and maintaining its sacramental life. Where the Catholic Church has seen some numerical success in recent years has been largely seen through incorporating Catholics who have recently immigrated to the UK—both from Europe and the developing world.[61]

'Deconstructing' traditional churches

Concern for the poor has always been a key feature of churches with a more 'liberal' theological persuasion. It is common in such churches to adopt popular social justice causes such as Fairtrade, environmentalism or homelessness. Numerous largely middle class liberal churches are characterised by this type of concern, which influences their preaching, their activism and their liturgy. However, this seems rarely to result in meaningful attempts to integrate those struggling with serious poverty into the main life of the church.

However, a few more radical advocates of this theological approach have attempted something much more ambitious. They have tried to rework the culture and structure of existing congregations in poor areas in an attempt to reach the poor. At a recent conference I heard one church leader describe how she felt she had needed to 'deconstruct' her church in order to achieve any sense of inclusiveness. She decided that the liturgy, music, preaching and structure of church meetings just did not work for those from deprived backgrounds who attended her church. Traditional non-conformity was not having much impact in her urban area. Her emphasis was on building an inclusive community for rich and poor together. The new format focused on very informal gatherings based on eating together and informal prayer, Bible reading and discussion. There are other churches following this path, but not that many. The focus of this type of church is to reconsider its middle class culture and traditional churchmanship and assess what of all this may prevent the church being able to embrace the poor in their locality. The theological centre of such churches tends to be a strong doctrine of the love of God for all people and the out-working of this tends to be strong community building across all sectors of the community—with a robust invitation to link with the church congregation.

This process of 'deconstruction' is a radical attempt to address a vital issue. Church leaders involved certainly don't lack courage and commitment. What are the outcomes? These are hard to measure. The charity Church Action on Poverty[62] is monitoring such strategies but reports that they have not often been attempted and that clear-cut trends and outcomes are hard, as yet, to determine.[63]

Redeploying resources—denominational tactics to stem church decline in poor areas

Numerical church decline in the UK affects most parts of the church. This decline is of concern to all churches—but of particular concern to those denominations, such as Methodists and the URC, whose numerical decline has been particularly steep. That decline has led to closure of many churches and chapels over the past few decades. One particular challenge has been to maintain churches in poor, largely urban, areas.

This has led to some rethinking at a national level. Here are two examples.

One outcome has been the process of linking together (and often amalgamating) struggling churches from different denominations into a single Local Ecumenical Project (LEP).[64] An LEP is a formal agreement between two churches to work together or join together on a long term basis. This certainly helps in the short term as ministerial costs are shared and facility costs are reduced. However, most of those close to the process would admit (sometimes privately) that the movement towards LEPs has not stemmed the numerical decline in the longer term. It is usually more about managing diminishing resources than a springboard for a new missional approach towards the poor or anyone else.

The Church of Scotland has taken another approach to a similar challenge—this is the 'Priority Areas Programme'. Dozens of areas of social deprivation across Scotland are the basis for the programme, in which the aim is to bring about 'a reinvigorated and sustainable worshipping people and community life in all 65 priority area parishes'.[65] It is an ambitious programme that has significant finances allocated to it. There is an emphasis on creatively reusing church buildings, supporting paid ministerial leadership and finding practical ways of engaging with the social needs of each area. The programme has certainly strengthened and encouraged struggling congregations in poor areas across Scotland. Its missional impact on the poorest sectors of those communities is harder to assess from the available evidence.

'Fresh Expressions'—rethinking local church

In 2004 the Anglican and Methodist churches launched an attempt to re-imagine local church life and outreach through the 'Fresh Expressions' movement.[66] Other denominations are now partners in this initiative. This is an attempt to encourage local churches to form new worshipping communities that are culturally attractive and relevant to groups of people who are not currently drawn to the local church in its regular patterns of worship and church life. Hundreds of new projects have been undertaken in different formats: Cafe Church, Messy Church, Youth Church, Mid-week Church, Child-focused church ... and many more.[67] The Church Army's extensive research into 'Fresh Expressions' was published in 2016 and gave a detailed analysis of the outworkings of this significant trend in developing 'missional churches'. A number of encouraging trends were observed including the diversity of projects, the growing number of projects and the direct engagement with many people previously not worshipping regularly in a local church.

However, for our specific purpose two things are noteworthy.

Firstly, there is still ongoing debate about the extent to which many forms of 'Fresh Expressions' can be equated to the New Testament model of local church. This is an important biblical and contextual question that helps us to move beyond looking at numbers of people engaged to the sort of community they are engaging with. Significantly, according to the recent research, many attenders of 'Fresh Expressions' projects say they are often unclear that it is supposed to be a worshipping church as such.[68]

The second point is that research indicates that the 'Fresh Expressions' movement has not, in general, had a big impact on reaching the poorest communities in the country. To be fair, this was never the primary aim. The reason for this fact is not hard to find. Most churches adopting the 'Fresh Expressions' approach are not in deprived communities to start with—so they are unlikely to reach people in such areas by this methodology.

Focusing on social action

This is the priority of most evangelical churches across the denominations. Many have been willing to respond to social need on a project basis. During the past decade numerous types of social action projects have arisen to address many needs and those projects have been adopted by more and more churches across the country. However, such churches usually do not have any plans to do anything more than to be active in social action. The rest of their church life continues much as before and there is little expectation that those being helped by their projects are likely to get engaged with their community or their faith in any spiritually significant way. Such churches are, however, generally content with this situation. They are doing their bit, as they see it, to alleviate poverty and help those in their community. It can also be the case that they have become content with this because their experience tells them that those who turn to Christ after accessing social action projects are few and far between. Disappointment can lead to settling for less.

Indeed, one subtle outcome of this approach is the gradual lowering of expectations concerning the potential impact of social action projects on the recipients. It is noticeable to me in conversation with social action project volunteers all over the country that there is often little expectation of significant personal change for their 'clients'. Also, there is often very little attempt to link them to the relational networks of the church or its evangelistic activities. It seems to me that this trend has been on the increase as significant social action projects have become routine in many churches over the past decade.

Recent research carried out by Word on the Streets in association with Church Action on Poverty and Jubilee+ has identified the extent to which the UK church is, for the most part, still firmly middle class in its internal culture and its approach to reaching the poor in their communities.[69] When that middle class culture is unchallenged the most likely outworking of the church's approach to poverty is to confine its activity to social action projects alone.

Widening the reach of middle class churches

Some churches have not been content to just engage with social action. They also want to build a significant relational bridge between those who they are helping and the life of the church. They feel a sense of responsibility for the spiritual welfare of those they are helping. Sometimes there might be offers to pray for people. Sometimes there might be invitations to social events or guest services. In some cases there are invitations to outreach events and evangelistic courses such as Christianity Explored or Alpha. In this way some individuals and families have crossed over from being helped to being on a spiritual journey and joining a church community. This can be an exciting relational and spiritual journey. It can work well and some churches actively encourage this process. However, it is also a risky journey. If the largely middle class church is unwilling to modify its culture, there will be challenges. Also, if those making the journey into the heart of that community come from significantly different class, race or economic backgrounds—relational issues will often arise. For example, misunderstandings between different groups of people are very easy to find: one church leader from a working class background explains that the working class are straight-talking but the middle class see them as rude, whereas the middle class are polite, but the working class see them as two-faced or dishonest. Widening the reach of middle class churches is not easy to do unless the church consciously decides to empower the sub-culture of the incoming group. The only way this is going to happen is by people getting to know one another and becoming friends. Why not ask the incoming Middle Eastern group to cook a meal for the church—and teach the participants some of their customs as they eat, or tell stories of their homeland? Or go for a gentle, family-friendly, walk, followed by a picnic tea? Find ways to create activities where the existing congregation is able to learn something from the incoming group, rather than creating a culture of disempowered recipients of charity.

I know a church that specialises in providing free English lessons for immigrant groups in their area. These lessons are well led and popular. The church also emphasises building relationships with the participants. Friendships develop as the courses go on. The classes take place in the church building. This provides a good basis for inviting participants, as appropriate, to church events such as guest services and social events. The pastor reflects that this has been the most successful way in which his largely middle class church has widened its reach to welcome immigrant groups into church life and to introduce them to the gospel message. Some have responded. They have found a home within the church and the church has learnt many things about welcoming and integrating these new people.

A friend of mine commented on the significant change to the Sunday congregation in her firmly middle class church after it started reaching out strategically to the homeless through a particular local project. Later on there was an influx of foreign medical workers who had moved to the UK to work in a particular group of hospitals. Many had Christian backgrounds and were seeking a church. Then, later again, the church began to be connected to local refugee/asylum support projects. In this way, over a few years the previously all white middle class city church changed to become multi-ethnic and socially diverse as a variety of newcomers joined the community of the church and embraced personal faith in Christ. Such a change was not without its challenges, but the pastoral leaders adapted the culture of the church step-by-step to enable incomers to feel part of the community.

Let's reflect on this story to see what we can learn. The most obvious observation is that circumstances played a key role. It so happened that the church encountered a variety of new social groups in a similar time period for a variety of different reasons. No one planned this—it just happened. Proximity can be a key to change. Those involved in the church at the time note that a culture of openness and welcome was encouraged by the church leaders. A welcoming atmosphere and generous hospitality went a long way to bring about social integration.

Another key factor was that there were a few influential activists in the church who led by example and were mostly involved in related social projects. The combination of key activists with a strong and sympathetic leadership often opens the way to the growth of social and ethnic diversity in local churches. In this case they pulled together—and it worked. Two things that the church leaders also did which helped this process are worth mentioning. Firstly, they taught on God's heart for the poor in their preaching. Secondly, they often called on the church members to give financially to help particular people in need such as the homeless or asylum seekers.

While it is vital we respond to the changing circumstances around us, just as the church mentioned above did, we must also be aware of the deep-seated issues that may have existed in our communities for a long time. Part of transforming our churches to reach the poor around us, requires us to know the area well and consider appropriate ways to address key needs. When I (Natalie) started working for my local church, one of the first things I did was meet with local decision-makers—the chief of police, our MP, the leader of the council, the head of community safety, etc.—to ask them what *they* felt the biggest issues facing the town were, in terms of deprivation, and what *they* would like to see churches such as mine contribute to helping local people in need.

Multiple congregations

Some mission-orientated churches have recognised that people from the poorer parts of town are not likely to join their church— nor are their foodbank clients or others facing poverty. Maybe they live too far away, or the buses on Sunday don't work for them, or they don't cope well with coming to a strong and established church community on a Sunday. For such churches there is an alternative. They can start satellite congregations in different parts of their town or area. Such congregations can be thoroughly culturally embedded in the areas or social groups they are designed to reach, but they can also draw upon the resources of the central church in terms of oversight, finance and practical help on the ground when needed. Such satellite congregations depend on good leadership, but they also often find resourcing their work a particular challenge.

Here are three contrasting examples of multiple congregational churches.

The first example comes from a church I (Martin) know in which one of the pastors has pioneered a ministry to the homeless and recovering addicts. He has seen remarkable breakthrough among this group. Some have embraced the life of faith in Christ— others are spiritual seekers. This group found it very hard to fit in with the regular Sunday congregation due to the vastly different life experiences and issues they had faced. So it was amicably agreed that they should form a satellite congregation of the church, overseen by the same pastors, but meeting separately from the main congregation on most occasions. This satellite congregation has proved a positive experience for those involved. Care has been taken, however, to ensure that there is as much relational contact as possible between the two congregations even though they meet separately. This has been done through social events, personal friendships and church activities. In this way, a wider unity between them has been maintained. Also, some more established members of the satellite congregation have chosen to join the main congregation.

What are some of the lessons learnt in running this satellite congregation? Three come to mind from discussions with the leaders involved. Firstly, the importance of sticking to the task over the long haul. Long-term commitment counts for a lot among a social group whose lives may change only slowly. Leaders need to be committed over a long time, but so do a core of members whose priority it is to reach a needy social group. Secondly, a focus on high relational content of the meetings and other social interactions is vital. A quick ten-minute cup of coffee at the end of the weekly service doesn't generally do the trick. Social times are a key part of any service—and they need plenty of time. Thirdly, the importance of robust preaching. Dumbing down the preaching has not been the approach taken. Preaching is fairly short, but very direct and practical. Storytelling in preaching is particularly important. Strong biblically-based talks with a single well illustrated point tend to achieve the best impact.

The second example comes from a church that was, until recently, a largely white, middle class church. It has been successful in attracting numbers of Eritrean immigrants (among others). However, such is the cultural and linguistic challenge of accommodating the Eritreans into the main Sunday meeting that it has been decided that they should have their own congregation, for the time being. The new congregation is still seen as part of the main church and is overseen by the same pastors. Also, some of the Eritreans attend the main church meetings as well as their own. However, for the practical purpose of creating meaningful congregational life, it seems easier for them to have their own meeting. This may change over time as the Eritreans become more strongly integrated socially and as their English language skills increase. Even now the second generation of the Eritreans are becoming more and more integrated with the main church congregation.

The third example concerns a thriving Anglican church in a pleasant and affluent village with a working class estate nearby. Hardly anyone from the estate ventures into the village to attend the church—such is the cultural divide—so the church has started and resourced a satellite congregation on the estate with the sole aim of reaching out to those who are spiritually open, but who are unlikely ever to go to the middle class parish church in the village.

I recently spoke at a large, vibrant church in a large English town that meets in a new building on the edge of town. This church is very active in the community and some of the poorest people in the town visit the church building to receive help from various social action projects. Most of these people come from a very poor district at the other end of town. So it has been suggested that a satellite congregation should be established in the poor district. As I write, members of the church are preparing to relocate to live in the poor district in preparation for the establishment of a satellite congregation in due course.

Sending urban missionaries

The unique work of Andy Hawthorne and The Message Trust,[70] based in Manchester, was developed in the late 1980s out of passionate concern for the welfare of young people in inner city areas. The initial focus was on the evangelism of young people, but over time The Message also began to address issues of social justice and widened its scope to reach out to whole communities, not just young people. The Message has for some years been sending trained teams of 'urban missionaries' to go to live and work in deprived urban areas. This broader initiative is called the Eden network.[71] At the time of writing over forty Eden teams have been sent, comprising over four hundred urban missionaries. These are impressive numbers in the UK context. The Eden network seeks to find partner churches in the communities in which it begins to operate.

This methodology is significant for our purposes. It is rooted in evangelical convictions about the centrality of the gospel, about preaching and about gathering converts. It also has a strong social justice dimension. The work of The Message and the associated Eden network is borne out of an evangelistic motivation and it is focused specifically on the urban poor. However, it does not identify church planting as a central goal of its evangelistic mission. As a result, the long-term success of its evangelism of the poor will depend to a great extent on the nature of the partnerships with pre-existing local churches that it is able to develop.

The Message is not the only movement to have adopted this type of methodology, but it is by far the biggest and most influential.

Church planting among the poor

The most radical response to the challenge to be a church for the poor is to plant brand new churches in deprived areas! These churches will be more than satellite congregations, since their aim will be to develop ultimately into self-supporting churches with their own fully equipped leadership teams, and more than urban mission teams. It is well known that few churches are flourishing in the most deprived areas of the UK. The long-term trend towards churches being more numerous and larger in middle class areas has already been noted. Many estates are without a church at all. The doors have closed on many churches in such areas during the past fifty years. For example, in Scotland many of the most deprived estates ('schemes') used to have Mission Halls built there by wealthy churches in the more affluent districts nearby. Many of these Mission Halls have now closed.

This type of church planting is not easy. It takes significant leadership skills to build a church community from scratch in a deprived area. But the good news is that pioneer leaders are doing it all over the UK. I've been involved with this process myself as a church leader. I know lots of people involved in it right now. I'm privileged to hear their stories. The exciting thing about this process is that the culture of the local community can more easily be properly represented in the new church, thus making it more effective in reaching people right there in the locality.

Church planting in deprived areas is a giant step towards realising the vision of being a church for the poor. However, such churches, once established, must not become culturally separated from other churches in their towns or cities. Being a church for the poor is not a niche calling for a few; it is the responsibility of all churches. Churches need to partner together to reach out to the most needy communities whether they be white working class, immigrant communities, black or Asian communities or the rural poor.

One of the most radical attempts at church planting among the poor has been undertaken by Mez McConnell and the '20schemes' movement in Scotland.[72] Currently, McConnell leads Niddrie Community Church in Edinburgh.[73] Niddrie is one of the most deprived areas of the city. McConnell plans to facilitate the planting of twenty new churches in Scotland's poorest urban areas over the next few years. His work has inspired similar church planting in other parts of the UK.

McConnell and others like him have a strong desire not only to reach the poor for Christ in their own social environments, but to create a culture of discipleship in their churches. Such a strategy has the advantage of enabling leaders among the poor to emerge and begin to function in leadership roles within the church. This is a vital aspect of becoming a church for the poor. Recently, while visiting a fairly rich city church to preach there, I had a pleasant reminder of this wonderful process of personal transformation. During the service, the worship leader gave a brief description of his background. He had been an immigrant to the UK who spent some years as a semi-alcoholic pub singer. His lifestyle was rough. Then he found faith in Christ. He is now an established member of the wider leadership of his church. There are many like him—and many, many more who need to be given the opportunity of discipleship and leadership training.

Radical church planting of the type described here is based on robust evangelical theological convictions about gospel preaching, the process of conversion, the vital role of the local church, the importance of personal discipleship—and the priority of reaching the poor for Christ. This goes far beyond the 'social action culture' that is so prevalent in much contemporary evangelicalism. In fact, social action itself forms only a modest part of this model. The top priority here is making disciples among the poorest communities in the country.

These church planting initiatives provide an amazing opportunity for the wider church. This is not a specialist work that does not concern the wider church—on the contrary it is of central importance to all churches. Some church leaders are called to move to such churches from more comfortable settings. Some church members are called to move into these types of church planting areas to help build these new churches. Some are called to pray consistently for these churches. Some churches are called to give significant amounts of money to help these financially poor churches resource their local mission to the poorest sectors of British society.

ELEVEN

BUILDING A CHURCH FOR THE POOR—KEYS

It's time now to turn for a moment from our discussion about what is happening on the ground in the UK in the quest to build a church for the poor. Let's step back and ask ourselves what foundations we are building upon. What vision of church do we carry in our minds and hearts? And to what extent is this vision shaped by the Bible?

We can easily be driven by a sense of responsibility, or even guilt, in our quest to respond to the needs of the poor in our communities. However, this will never be a strong enough basis for a long-term and radical Christian contribution to the issue of poverty.

So let's turn back to the pages of the New Testament. We have already noted the radical engagement with the poor that characterised the early churches of the apostolic era described in the book of Acts (chapter 3). Let's dig a bit deeper into this narrative to try to identify the foundations that underlay the amazing care for the poor conducted by the church in its earliest days.

As I (Martin) read through the New Testament I've noticed four key foundations in the early church's care for the poor.

Practical care

Jesus demonstrated practical care for those in need. He gave them time, he was compassionate towards them, he healed them, he comforted them and he even fed them. He expected his disciples to follow in his footsteps and they did so from the very earliest days of the church. We have already discussed this point in chapter three. We noted there that a summary of the outlook of the early apostles on this issue was given in Galatians 2:10: 'All they asked was that we should continue to remember the poor, the very thing I had been eager to do all along.' We can be sure that the churches of the New Testament reached out to the poor in their localities wherever they were across the Roman Empire. An awareness of this priority and focus has become increasingly understood today as a key to our own engagement with poverty.

Advocacy

It is the book of James that brings the issue of advocacy to the fore. We looked at the context of this in chapter three. Here's a quick reminder: James was a senior church leader based in Jerusalem. His letter was written to scattered Jewish Christian groups who had been forced by persecution and economic factors to leave their homes and settle in other parts of the Roman Empire. James wrote a circular letter to encourage and guide them. He was aware that these Jewish Christians were now living in some very unjust societies and were even victims of social injustice themselves on some occasions as a result of their economic vulnerability and their Christian faith. James was particularly aware of the widespread and ruthless exploitation of farm labourers by exploitative landowners in some places. He must have heard first-hand accounts of this from some of the scattered Christians. In his letter he has this to say:

> Now listen, you rich people, weep and wail because of the misery that is coming on you. Your wealth has rotted, and moths have eaten your clothes. Your gold and silver are corroded. Their corrosion will testify against you and eat your flesh like fire. You have hoarded wealth in the last days. Look! The wages you failed to pay the workers who mowed your fields are crying out against you. The cries of the harvesters have reached the ears of the Lord Almighty. You have lived on earth in luxury and self-indulgence. You have fattened yourselves in the day of slaughter. You have condemned and murdered the innocent one, who was not opposing you. (James 5:1-6)

This is the sort of passage that makes you take a deep breath. It is strong language. It is not necessarily politically correct! However, it is advocacy pure and simple. James, a church leader, speaks up for a particular group of oppressed and exploited labourers. He is concerned for their needs and he is taking up their case. This is the heart of advocacy and is part of the mandate of the New Testament church. It strongly echoes the role of the Old Testament prophets who often took up the case of those who were being socially or economically exploited in ancient Israel (e.g. Amos 2:6-8).

If the church of the New Testament era took the opportunity to speak up for the disempowered and marginalised, then so should we! And the process starts with those most closely associated with our churches in our localities. Advocacy can be complicated, but it is important. It is also prophetic. Advocacy speaks of a God who cares for the oppressed and who will bring oppressors to account. It is an important part of church ministry to have an advocacy role in our society. Sometimes this is done on a national level such as the current emphasis in the church on campaigning over the modern slavery of human trafficking. However, for local churches seeking to build a church for the poor, advocacy can be done on a one-to-one basis, such as the church I know that takes cases of unjust treatment of benefits claimants directly to the local JobCentre Plus to explain the injustice of a decision or a sanction.

Advocacy can also involve churches working closely with local organisations to help them bring about justice. For example, one church we are familiar with has worked alongside the police in their town to help them understand the issue of human trafficking. The main police officer in contact with the members of the church involved in this ministry credits them with changing the perception of local police officers from treating those who have been trafficked as criminals to treating them as victims. This is advocacy. This is the church not only fighting for justice, but working with others to help them bring about justice too. The prophet Ezekiel asked who would stand in the gap (Ezek. 22:30). Advocacy is about standing in the gap between those who could easily be oppressed or discarded or written off and those who might treat others in this way. It can include mentoring a child at risk of exclusion from school or lobbying the government to change legislation affecting workers' rights. We can shy away from advocacy sometimes because it can seem too big, but we are called to 'speak up for those who cannot speak for themselves, for the rights of all who are destitute [...] defend the rights of the poor and needy' (Prov. 31:8-9).

Evangelism

Jesus was unambiguous. His 'manifesto' in the synagogue at Nazareth at the outset of his public ministry had this opening statement: 'The Spirit of the Lord is on me, because he has anointed me to proclaim good news to the poor' (Luke 4:18). Among all the other wonderful things that Jesus did he specifically proclaimed 'good news' to the poor. We should not sentimentalise this statement. The 'good news' was not primarily about improving their self-confidence or even just demonstrating God's love for them. No, the good news was about the kingdom of God, which had just arrived in power and which demanded a response. It demanded repentance from personal sin and an active response of faith in the person and work of Jesus (Mark 1:15). It also required a willingness to identify with Jesus as one of his disciples even when that was an unpopular and costly thing to do (Mark 8:34-35). Jesus called people to respond to his message of 'good news'. Such a response was public and clear-cut. It involved changed belief and a changed lifestyle.

Were the poor exempted from the need to respond to the good news of the gospel? Far from it. Jesus made the same call to repentance, faith and discipleship to everyone. His message is universal and everyone, whatever their status in life, is called to truly believe in him to receive eternal salvation (John 3:16-21).

The early church had the same conviction. They preached the same message to everyone—to Jew and Gentile, to men and women, to slaves and to the free. Significantly, Paul noted that the poor were well represented in the churches (1 Cor. 1:26) and James stated that God has a particular desire to see the poor enter into his eternal salvation (James 2:5).

This is a big challenge to us. There has been a noticeable tendency in the UK church to focus on social action at the expense of personal evangelism, or vice-versa. A dangerous divide has accidentally arisen in the practice of some churches, which will ultimately undermine any possibility of being truly a church for the poor. When social action alone becomes the priority, the church sooner or later becomes virtually indistinguishable from a secular charity or social welfare organisation. It loses its distinctive message and identity. The story of the Salvation Army is a stark reminder of this trend. As we saw in chapter four, William Booth founded the Salvation Army because he became frustrated with the failure of the church of his day to reach the working classes and the urban poor in Victorian England. He combined radical social action with fervent evangelism. He would not allow anything to drive a wedge between practical care for the poor and his concern for their spiritual welfare. Over the years the Salvation Army has found it a great challenge to live out the radical philosophy of its founder. The risk today is that the Salvation Army is mostly known to wider society for its social projects and not for its gospel message.

An immediate concern may come to mind right now. You may be wondering if I am proposing manipulating vulnerable people as we help them. Should we present the gospel to people who may feel obliged to try to respond to its message due to their sense of indebtedness to us? It is unethical to be manipulative. We must be clear on that point. However, we do need to provide sensitive and suitable ways of inviting the poor on a spiritual journey of discovery that will involve the possibility, in the right context, of explaining the full gospel message to them and inviting a response.

The New Testament makes clear that the gospel has to be presented directly to people (Matt. 28:19, Acts 1:8, Rom. 1:16-17). People cannot pick up the gospel message by merely being influenced by the example of Christians living sacrificially and loving the poor. We dare not modify the priority of presenting the gospel to people. We must not fall for such half-truths as 'we preach the gospel with our lives and use words if necessary'. This sounds attractive, but it is not a truly biblical perspective. We need both to live out our faith with our lives and take every appropriate opportunity to explain our faith to those outside the church— whoever they are. This includes the poor.

Let me tell you the story of my friend Jim. Jim had had a messed up life and became a drug addict as a young man. He ended up in a drug rehabilitation centre in our town. Our church had strong links with the centre and, for some years, ran support groups for those wanting to develop the skills to lead addiction-free lives. Jim initially came to our church meetings while still on a

rehab programme and on the first Sunday he heard me preach on
God's desire to 'restore the years the locusts have eaten'. He was
very moved by the occasion. Soon afterwards he came to one of
those support groups. During the group he heard about the Alpha
course and was keen to come. Then on the Alpha course he heard
the gospel explained and quickly made an enthusiastic response to
Christ. Several years of discipleship followed as Jim struggled to
throw off the legacy of all the problems of his past life. He made
steady progress despite occasional setbacks. He was subsequently
able to hold down jobs and build a new life. Now, many years later,
Jim is a key member of a church plant in a major city and he has
important responsibilities in its outreach. Jim needed more than a
few tips on how to live an addiction-free life. He needed the transforming message of the gospel. He responded and was changed
from within.

Paul describes the gospel as 'the power of God that brings
salvation to everyone who believes' (Rom. 1:16). This is a vital
statement. The gospel has power to change people. It is a transforming message. It is confirmed by the powerful work of the Holy
Spirit in the lives of individuals who hear it. We unleash the power
of God by explaining the good news of Christ to the poor and
marginalised.

Discipleship

Jesus saw practical discipleship as vital to the wellbeing of the
church. In order to understand this we need to take a fresh look at
his commission to his apostles as recorded in Matthew:

> All authority in heaven and on earth has been
> given to me. Therefore go and make disciples of all
> nations, baptising them in the name of the Father
> and of the Son and of the Holy Spirit, and
> teaching them to obey everything I have
> commanded you. And surely I am with you always,
> to the very end of the age. (Matt. 28:18-20)

Discipleship is training people to live effectively as Christians. Jesus didn't just want new converts to be baptised—he wanted them to become disciples. This cannot happen unless converts become part of local churches and grow in their faith in the context of community life, worship, fellowship, teaching, communion and involvement in the day-to-day life of a church. However, discipleship is more than any of these things. Discipleship involves active mentoring of new or less experienced Christians. Such mentoring will include Bible teaching, prayer, personal sharing, accountability, and opportunities to grow in the gifts each person has. Meaningful discipleship is often missing in our churches, yet it is necessary in order to build strong churches and to help new Christians to grow in their faith and be effective in their lives.

Now let's apply this to the poor. Many poor people make meaningful responses to the gospel. One church leader working among the poor recently said to me: 'My experience is that the poor are much more open to the gospel than other groups in the UK.' This is true. However, once people decide they want to follow Christ, there are often major lifestyle or cultural issues to address. This is where discipleship comes in. The poor need to be discipled just like everyone else needs to be discipled. This can only happen if they are meaningfully connected to local churches that believe in and practice New Testament discipleship. This is a challenging process, but needs to be undertaken if we are to see a church for the poor in the UK. One of the wonderful outcomes of this process is that some of those who first come to the church as those in need end up taking positions of responsibility and leadership in those churches.

Let me end this chapter with the story of a friend of mine. His name is Soroush and he is an Iranian who sought asylum in the UK after converting to Christ in Iran and facing serious persecution.[74] As an asylum-seeker, Soroush was welcomed into a church in the north-east of England. He was helped practically and became a member of that church. Soon he displayed gifts of leadership and began to help with caring for fellow Iranians and other immigrants who were linked with the church. Then over time he was recognised as an elder in the church. Soroush first encountered the church as a poor asylum-seeking immigrant. Now he is a recognised member of the pastoral leadership team.

Building a church for the poor will ultimately lead to leaders emerging from among the poor. This is a powerful sign of God's grace to a watching world.

TWELVE

BUILDING A CHURCH FOR THE POOR—CAPACITY

Church leaders have a hard job. I (Martin) used to run the local church ministers' gathering in our town. Every month we would meet in a different church and listen to the story of what was happening in that church and the minister would tell us of the problems he or she was facing. It was an opportunity to share openly among supportive friends. It was amazing to me to hear of the range of challenges being faced day by day: pastoral complexities, denominational problems, financial shortfalls, buildings issues, legal challenges, people leaving the church, family difficulties, boredom, discouragements, temptations ...

Twenty-first century Britain is a tough place in which to be a church leader. The pundits tell us that the church is in terminal decline, while secular values undermine the gospel message and the lure of materialism makes for much nominal Christianity. There are people who try to marginalise the church or keep its voice quiet, and there are people who simply ignore us.

All this makes for a real capacity problem when it comes to building a church for the poor. For many church leaders, this is a bridge too far. Survival and maintenance are their priority. Donations to favoured charities? Yes. A collecting point for the local foodbank? No problem. A Christmas collection for the homeless night shelter? Great idea. A church for the poor—no, that's more than we can consider for this church, thank you. We simply haven't got the resources.

Let's look at it another way. There's an old saying that 'God's work, done in God's way, never lacks God's resources.' I've got this saying pinned up on the notice board in my office. Just to remind me. I've been a church leader for over twenty-five years and have discovered through experience that there is frequently a remarkable process by which resources become available to a church which takes seriously the apostolic mandate to 'remember the poor'.

So what resources do we need? There are four vital ones to consider.

Human resources

People are almost always the key resource we need—and the people who count most in the first instance are actually the church leaders themselves! A heart for the poor must be within them if any church is ever going to be effective in being a church for the poor. This may seem obvious, but in my experience the real problem has been the lack of commitment by the church leader(s) to care for the poor. To some it is a secondary issue, to others it is too challenging, and to others it is a distraction from other priorities. The remedy is quite simple—a clear biblical perspective on the priority of the poor in God's kingdom and the ministry of the church. From a biblical perspective we then need to move to identify a sense of the particular callings and opportunities open to each church in their particular area. Once this is done then comes the biggest challenge of all—to step out of our comfort zones and begin to work with the poor. Leaders create opportunities for their churches. They open doors—or they leave them closed. As I write this chapter I have just returned from a visit to a lively new and growing church in an urban area near a major centre for human trafficking. At the time of my visit the church leaders were considering opening up an outreach to sex workers in the area, many of whom were linked to local trafficking networks. The potential project leader had emerged, the need was apparent, the resources could be gathered. The decision was in the hands of the church leaders; would they open the doors or leave them closed?

Once a church leader or leadership team is convinced that the Holy Spirit is calling their church, in some specific way, to be a church for the poor, then another vital stage in the process is underway. In the New Testament there is a wonderful pattern of church leadership that involves both overseers (or pastors) and deacons. Read 1 Timothy 3:1-13 and Philippians 1:1 to get a feel for this New Testament pattern. Pastors are intended to function in teams and to take the overall responsibility for the whole church community. New Testament deacons, on the other hand, are leaders in specific areas of the life of the church.

Interestingly, the first deacon-type team mentioned in the New Testament was formed of seven men who were given the responsibility of handling the daily distribution of food among the poorer sections of the church in Jerusalem (Acts 6:1-6). They did this on behalf of the main church pastors. Social action requires leadership and organisation. This can rarely be provided effectively by church pastors as they have numerous other responsibilities. On the other hand, the church leaders cannot easily or safely hand over social action projects to enthusiasts and activists alone. There is a vital leadership element required to build teams, shape projects and effectively care for those we are seeking to reach. This is the work of a deacon—someone called, equipped and able to work in social action while being appropriately linked to church pastors and the main life of the church. In my experience the key is to find suitably skilled deacons. Many projects can't really get off the ground or develop well until suitable leadership is put in place. Once this has been done, then activists are usually not hard to find.

My observation over the years has been that if the biblical pattern of leadership is not followed there will usually be a major problem. Here's what I have noticed: in a typical local church the leaders are busy with the many responsibilities of church leadership. Church members begin to lobby them over some particular social need. The leaders then feel under pressure to do something about the need. They have neither the skill, the time, nor the inclination to get involved themselves, so they simply pass the responsibility back to those who are concerned. The message they send out is—you get on and do something about this social need. So the lobbyists become the activists. However, their activism creates problems for themselves and tensions within the church. Everyone is uneasy, and the project gets into difficulties.

Bringing a deacon into the mix in the early stages avoids this altogether. Deacons have the spiritual stature, leadership abilities and engagement with the specific social need in question to be able to build teams and mobilise activists in an effective way for both the work in hand and the wider church community.

Financial resources

Caring for needy people usually costs money—and money is in short supply in most churches. A friend of mine who pastors a large church with extensive commitments to social action is clear on the best approach to money: 'I think money follows vision, so if you set a clear vision finances will follow.' His church is a living example of this reality as church members have regularly donated generously to many projects. Social action and care for the poor needs to be central in the vision of a local church. Church members need to feel a sense of ownership of the work that is being done. Such ownership will lead to financial generosity to support the work as required. For most Christians, giving to the local church is a central part of their thinking. However, they tend to consider giving to the poor in a separate category—and rightly so. The church needs to capitalise on this willingness to give over and above what is given to the central church funds. In addition to this, some churches have business people with significant assets who are often willing to sponsor particular projects. Business people and other wealthy church members often find that they don't easily fit into local churches. Churches are often unsympathetic to the needs and outlook of heavily committed business people. However, such people are potentially a great asset to the church in a variety of different ways. Many will respond favourably to being involved in social action projects by making significant financial contributions, helping with the practical management of such projects or simply by volunteering their expertise and energy. This is one reason why we need to build truly diverse churches, not merely multiple gatherings of people who all look, act and sound the same.

In many areas of care for the poor it is also possible to gain financial support from outside the church. This can come in many forms: one-off donations, grant funding, provision of facilities by outside agencies, local authority support, etc. Sometimes it is worth designating a particular person to look out for these types of opportunity and capitalise on them. One strategy that has been used more and more recently is to create a separate charity or company linked to the church that is responsible for the social action projects. This can have the benefit of more easily attracting outside funding and thus increase the financial resources of social action linked to the church.

At the end of the day, social action has to be carefully budgeted for in any local church. Commitments to projects need to be measured carefully against available budgeted resources. There is a skill of both spiritual leadership and practical financial management involved in making wise decisions that will enable sustainable social action projects. It is vital that those responsible for financial decision-making and management are envisioned by the objectives of the social action being undertaken by their church.

Physical resources

Generally speaking, churches need buildings to function to their maximum capacity. I spent a lot of time during my years as a church leader being responsible for a large building project, which we undertook shortly after I had become the church pastor. Having purchased an old Territorial Army training base, it took us over fifteen years to refurbish, extend and adapt the building to meet all our needs. Then, when we thought it was all complete, we found out that the site next door to our building was for sale, so we stepped out in faith again and bought that too! This gave us three buildings on our campus giving us a wide range of options.

As a result of these many years of experience with church building projects, I have spent a lot of time talking to other church leaders about issues relating to buildings. The most common scenario is renovation and changing the use of the available space. However, the purchase or leasing of new buildings is also often what is in view. Through all this experience I have come to realise how important the buildings we use and own are for a local church.

One thing I did not realise when I set out on the path of church leadership over twenty-five years ago, though, is that suitable buildings or premises can completely transform the capacity of a church to care for the poor. Our foodbank started out in a small storage room hidden away at the back of our church building. Now we have been able to dedicate one of our two new buildings to the foodbank. In fact, the size of the building is such that we can accommodate two other related social action projects in the same building, as well as being able to scale up our foodbank operation so that it effectively covers the whole town. New facilities have made all the difference.

So often it's facilities that determine what you can achieve.

Often church buildings are not very suitable for foodbanks, homeless drop-in facilities, mentoring groups, refugee support work or other similar projects. Generally church buildings are the only facilities available for our social action projects. While this can have its benefits (people coming to our church buildings), it can often be a constraint. For example, my (Natalie's) church building is on the outskirts of town, with limited public transport links. In order to try to solve this accessibility issue and other related difficulties, many churches have in recent years managed to obtain offices, meeting rooms, storage areas, joint use facilities, warehouses and even high street shop units as extra venues for use in their social action work.

Sometimes there is a need to think 'out of the box' and to be bold in seeking to find the facilities that are needed to enable churches to engage fully in social action. Here's a recent example I (Martin) came across. A Street Pastors organisation in a large town was struggling to find storage for their equipment and a place to use regularly as a base for their town centre night patrols. Discussions with local police and council officers led to the offer of a town centre shop premise for their use at a nominal rental. The use of this strategic and highly visible site enabled them to have a great base, excellent storage and a much higher public profile in their community.

Spiritual resources

The great risk about caring for the poor is that it all becomes about activism.

Doing, doing, doing …

We must take time to renew our spiritual resources if we are on the front line of care for those in need. This is a top priority. I have seen too many cases of emotional burnout as church leaders, project leaders and church members wilt under the pressure of constant front-line caring and giving. Balanced lifestyles are vital, otherwise we can be overwhelmed with the issues we are dealing with. Recreation matters. Personal devotion counts for a great deal. We have to be able to recharge our batteries.

Perhaps the most critical thing to keep coming back to is our motivation. Why are we doing what we do? Is it out of guilt? Or out of duty? If so, there is a danger of burnout. Everyone involved in social action needs to be strengthened by being sure they are doing things for the right reasons such as a genuine sense of calling and an awareness of the biblical basis for what they are doing.

Prayer is another vital issue. Churches need to be praying about their outreach to the poor. One pastor friend recently told me what his church does about prayer for their social action: 'We pray monthly as a church community and we have two weeks of prayer and fasting annually. Prayer is a very important aspect of breaking into our community and being a church that represents the locality we serve.'

As I write this I have just come from a church staff prayer meeting at which we were told about a forthcoming Saturday community day run by our child bereavement support project. The idea for the day is to provide a supportive and enjoyable environment for those families and children who we have been helping recently. Our whole staff team was able to gather and pray for the day—but not just for the day. We also prayed for the team who engage in this sacrificial and largely hidden ministry.

Prayer counts. Prayer sustains. Prayer energises.

Start small

I was once visiting a very small church plant in a poor area. It had about thirty members and met in a public hall. They had few resources and very little money, but the pastor and his wife had a great heart for the poor. They were aware of my involvement in social action so they broached the subject with me. They said, with some embarrassment, that they were only helping one poor person in their area—a widow in great need. I met the widow, whom they had housed and supported for some time. I encouraged them strongly. They had done exactly the right thing—they had started small. They had responded to an obvious need that had been brought to their attention, and this lady had become part of the church family.

They did what they could and they did it well.

So if you and your church are starting out on this journey of caring for the poor—start small. Do what you can. Don't be influenced by what bigger churches are doing in your area. You do what you can. Don't make the excuse that I sometimes hear: 'Our church is too small to help the poor—we will start getting involved in social action when we are a bit bigger.'

This same principle can apply to bigger churches too. I recently visited a large and wealthy church in an affluent part of the country. They asked me to address the issue of social action in their context. It soon became apparent that there was very little engagement with social action in the church despite its significant resources. My advice to them was to do what the small church I described above did—to start small.

So let's start small and start now.

From tiny seeds come great trees.

THIRTEEN

BUILDING A CHURCH FOR THE POOR—COUNTING THE COST

My (Martin's) life was solidly middle class. I was twenty-two. Newly married and newly qualified. I had just completed a university degree and teacher training. I had attended a large, vibrant, student-focused church while studying. My university friends were setting out on life as professionals, businessmen, civil servants, medics and lawyers.

I got a good job as a secondary school teacher, so my wife and I moved to a new area—Stoke-on-Trent in Staffordshire. Then came the question—what type of church should we join? There were plenty of lively Anglican, Pentecostal and Baptist options. We visited a few. Then a trusted friend suggested that we consider a new church that had started in the heart of the city. It was small and consisted almost entirely of local people who had lived in the area (known as The Potteries) all their lives. It could accurately be described as a working class church in its main culture. The Potteries has a strong local working class culture including its own vocabulary, distinctive accent, social history and sense of humour. There was a lot to learn!

My wife and I were warmly received by this church community—but we were quickly aware that we were cultural outsiders. Having someone with a degree in the church family was a novelty for them! We made some good friends and we came to love this church in the three years we lived in Stoke. However, we learnt a lot about culture and class in those formative years. We learnt new vocabulary. We adopted new eating habits—the words 'tea' and 'supper' took on new meanings. We learnt about preaching from the heart to the heart, even if the use of the text was a little theologically odd at times. We adapted to a different style of church meeting based mostly on the idea of an extended family in which people knew a great deal about each other's lives—rather than the more programme-driven, front-led churches we were used to.

We left Stoke after three formative years. Time passed. I gave up teaching and a few years later ended up as a church pastor. My experience in Stoke made me aware of the challenges that cultural outsiders can feel in a church. I remembered the feeling. This inspired me to always seek to find ways to help different social groups find a meaningful place in the church that I led. This process has had many outworkings, but one of the most important concerns how we seek to build a church for the poor.

Some years ago a Christian rehabilitation charity set up a residential centre in our town. They had a strong team and a firm Christian ethos. We were invited, as a church, to work alongside them and to find ways of forming a partnership between them and our church. After some time we came up with an idea: the church would host a support group for those who were further on in the rehab programme and who had made clear steps towards living an addiction-free life. This support group was designed to be a stepping stone towards the time when they would be leaving the local centre and living independently again. The idea was that we would discuss aspects of addiction-free living, life skills, seeking employment, etc. The support group would also be openly Christian and would offer prayer and spiritual input to those who were interested. Invitations to Alpha courses and other church events were to be made. Church volunteers were to be trained. One of my co-pastors was to host the group.

Such was the plan.

The group ran fairly successfully for a number of years. There were joys and sorrows along the way. It was a steep learning curve for our volunteers, some of whom did not remain in the team, while others came into their own and blossomed. No two meetings were the same. No two groups were the same.

For our volunteers, the biggest challenge was to bridge the cultural gap between their generally ordered and stable lives on the one hand and the chaotic and complicated lives of the course attenders on the other. Everything was a challenge: the use of language, time-keeping, dress code, social attitudes, expectations, understanding of how friendships operate, attitudes to authority ...

It was tough going at times—and not without tears, disappointment and discomfort for team members. Some realised that their desire to help was not matched by the emotional capacity needed or by sufficient relational flexibility to operate in this context.

Two stories illustrate some of the highs and lows of this season:

Evan attended the support group. He also showed up on Sundays at church. He seemed to be responding well to all the life skills discussion and the spiritual input. However, one day my phone rang at home out of working hours. It was our church manager—the church building had been broken into; could I come down quickly? I rushed down to see what had happened. All the offices had been broken into, the doors had been forced, the safes had been damaged, valuables had been stolen and thousands of pounds worth of damage inflicted. Then I realised that my office had come in for special treatment—and my filing cabinet had had all its four drawers broken into with the help of a crowbar. The police examined the site carefully. The officer in charge said to me quite emphatically: 'It looks to me like an inside job.' I was shocked. What an accusation to make against the church! I couldn't work it out.

A few days later the police were in touch again. Evan and his friend had been charged with the break in. They had been caught through fingerprinting. They ended up in prison convicted of numerous break-ins around the area. Our team visited Evan in prison—but on his release he left the area.

Many years have passed since then. The support group came to a natural end when the residential centre moved to another area. But my filing cabinet is still there in my office. The four crowbar marks are still there. The break in affected me deeply. Initially it felt like a form of violation, of abuse. Trust and love had been rejected and exploited. Our kindness had been violated in a very painful and personal way. We faced a choice. Do we withdraw from such risky acts of giving and protect the church by playing it a bit safer so that church members do not have to go through what I went through on that occasion? Or do we accept the risk of some painful situations arising and carry on doing what we know to be right?

We chose the latter—but not after some real heart searching. As a sign of my commitment I decided not to replace my filing cabinet. It is there as a symbolic reminder of the sometimes-bumpy road we walk when engaged in building a church for the poor. I can run my fingers over the crowbar marks anytime I need reminding that there is rarely joy without pain.

Yet on the other hand, there was Geoff. Geoff was in the support group at about the same time as Evan. He had fallen on hard times and ended up homeless on the streets of London. He had a few addiction issues too. One day a church worker from a London church got into conversation with Geoff on the streets. She invited him to her church to receive some help. Soon afterwards she recommended to Geoff that he apply to come to the rehabilitation centre in our town. Geoff came. Then he came to our support group. He quickly responded to the Christian message and became a committed believer. He's had a few ups and downs on the journey, but the outcome is that now he is married with a family, has held down a variety of jobs and has been involved in small group leadership in the church.

The day of Geoff's baptism will always be remembered as a red letter day for me. He asked for the lady from London to be one of the two baptisers—and I was the other one. She happily came up from London to share with our church in this great celebration of

Geoff's new life in Christ and his new church family. Even as I write these words I can feel the emotion as I recall this wonderful moment and as I think of the way Geoff has served and helped our church over the years since he joined us. I have watched his life develop, seen his family grow, and appreciated the quiet positive influence he has had on people around him.

Bringing together the rich and the poor, different classes, different races and different ages—that's the big social challenge for local churches. Becoming a church for the poor is a central and specific part of that challenge. Our church has made a few steps on the way, but there are a great many more steps to be taken. We are learning.

People do life together in different ways. People from working class or from poorer backgrounds often think and act differently to me. Over the years I have learnt to understand and appreciate such things as the power of storytelling, clothing styles that express personality rather than social aspiration, a lesser commitment to schedules and planning, a preference for cafes and pubs rather than coffee shops, a more direct style of talking, a higher tolerance of swearing and smoking, and a greater value put on people rather than possessions.

These are generalisations, but they are important ones. They tell us something about how we can see things differently and have different priorities according to our social background.

Every new cultural insight that helps to bridge the class and wealth divides is important for the mission of the church and particularly if we are to build a church for the poor. Each insight leads us to go on a sometimes uncomfortable journey of personal or cultural change. Joy and pain. Change isn't easy, but if we're committed to obedience to God's word, it may well be necessary.

People in church leadership like me always need to be reminded that this journey is a two-way process. It may be challenging for churches to widen their cultural reach and their capacity to embrace the poor. However, it is often even more challenging for those who embrace faith in Christ and want to belong, but are cultural outsiders. Natalie has shared something of her own journey elsewhere in this book. However, I can think of many people I know who have struggled along the road towards truly belonging to a church that had previously had little experience of relating to the poor or other cultural outsiders.

I think of a working man who couldn't read well and struggled on Sundays when Bible texts and other material appeared on the screen.

I think of an Eastern European family whose very long working hours and general lack of confidence in speaking English made it hard for them to integrate in the church.

I think of a lady who didn't like to speak in public and who was nervous when her home group leader asked her to read out a passage from the Bible. Just finding the passage was hard enough— let alone reading it.

I think of a man who found public meetings claustrophobic because he had spent so many years living on his own as he wrestled with addiction issues. He hung round the back of meetings and often went outside for a few minutes just to calm himself down.

The list could go on. There is both joy and pain for the poor and other outsiders as they seek to find their place in largely middle class churches, and the wisdom of Solomon needed for leaders seeking to help them.

Some years ago a homeless man came to our church with his dog. He got into discussion with the two stewards on duty as the service was about to start. The two stewards then came to me, as church leader, to ask what to do about him—and particularly his dog! There was (and is) a 'no animals' policy in the church building. The two men had opposing views. One argued that the man had to leave because he would not be parted from his dog and the dog wasn't welcome! The other man argued that the most important thing was that the man was welcomed and that we needed to turn a blind eye to the dog.

What should I do? I had five minutes to sort this out before I was due to start the church meeting. As I walked towards the man sitting at the back of the building I searched my mind and heart for an appropriate way forward, bearing in mind that even the two stewards did not agree on what to do! So I spoke warmly to the man and said that both he and the dog were welcome, but that the dog could not stay in the public main hall. I led him and his dog to my locked office, opened it up and prepared a bed for the dog in the corner of the office. I spoke kindly to the dog, settled it down, stroked it, and then persuaded the man to leave his dog there as I locked the office behind me. It was a risky plan—and I am sure you can quickly think of some of the risks that were going through my mind at that moment! However, I pressed on. I promised the homeless man that I would come to talk to him as soon as the service was over and that we would go to the office together to reunite the dog with his owner. Fortunately, the two stewards and the man agreed to the plan and left my office in peace. Afterwards the dog was happily returned to his owner having slept, apparently, throughout the whole service!

Another aspect to the pain and joy that accompanies care for the poor is that those who give themselves to it can feel like they are burning out. In Galatians 6:9 we instructed: 'Let us not become weary in doing good ...' But sometimes we do grow weary of it. Sometimes we feel bruised by the disappointment of seeing people return to their old patterns of behaviour, or of not seeing people come to Christ, or of seeing people turn to Jesus and then turn away again. Sometimes we grow weary of feeling like we have to persuade other Christians around us that caring for the poor is not an optional extra. The verses preceding Galatians 6:9 warn us to carry our own load, not to think of ourselves as anything other than what we are, and not to compare ourselves to others. This weariness in doing good often comes when we take our eyes off Jesus and instead focus on ourselves, other Christians around us, or the poor themselves.

We are called to be on a journey. There will be both joy and pain. There will be changes that need to be made. But the journey is worth it for the sake of building a church for the poor. We stay strong on the journey by walking closely with God and keeping our eyes fixed on Jesus. That is the only way to keep a merciful heart and to keep our vision burning.

FOURTEEN

CONCLUSION—WHERE DO WE GO FROM HERE?

Two trends are clear in recent years. Firstly, there has been a huge rise in concern among Christians to address issues of poverty directly and to take action to help those in most need. This has led to some of the remarkable developments we have discussed in this book. Secondly, there has been a trend among Christians towards less commitment to the local church. More and more Christians want faith without community, Christ without commitment to his people.

There is a painful paradox here that greatly concerns us.

As you will have already gathered, we, the authors, are as committed to the local church as we are to addressing the challenge of poverty and social exclusion. We need them both—we need heathy, strong churches as the basis on which to build a church for the poor.

We started this book by telling a little of our two very different personal stories. We tried to explain how we both felt called, in very different circumstances, to this great vision of a church for the poor.

As the book has gone along we have told you quite a few stories of people we have met along the way. We have also described some of the situations we have faced as we have worked on social action issues in our own two different churches. Our stories are a small part of a bigger story that we hear is being played out all over the country as more and more churches and individual Christians are sensing the increasing call to learn what it is to be a church for the poor.

Our book is in two parts. In it we have invited you to join us on a journey. A journey to play your part in enabling the development of a church for the poor across our nation.

In the first part of the book we looked at a lot of vital background issues. We engaged with the wider context in which our journey is set. We wrestled with the economics of poverty, we reflected on the different dimensions of poverty, we reconsidered the teachings of the New Testament, we delved into a bit of British church history, we reflected on some key aspects of our contemporary culture. Then we ended by inviting you to do some personal reflection about your own journey and about the things that have influenced your outlook on the poor.

Why have we included all this background material? Here's the main reason. As each of us travels around the country and as we work in our separate local churches we are constantly made aware of the many factors that subtly influence the thinking and actions of Christians in response to issues of poverty. In the first part of our book we have sought to address some of these issues very directly. We have found it challenging to relate to so many Christians who are struggling to know how to engage with poverty and all its consequences. So the first part of the book is all part of an orienteering process to enable us to focus on the powerful vision of a church for the poor. We need to know where we have come from before we can decide where we need to go.

In the second part of the book we have focused in some detail on local church life and on many specific issues. This is the practical part of the book. This is where the rubber hits the road. This is where we share the things we have learnt in our own churches and in our work helping churches around the country. This part of the book was informed by numerous helpful conversations with many friends up and down the country. All of them shared the same conviction: the church urgently needs to be a church for the poor. All of them are trying to work out that conviction in the context of their local communities. It has been inspiring to work alongside such people and to learn from them.

Underlying the second part of the book is a fervent passion for the local church. As stated above, we believe in the power of the local church. We believe it is by far the best means of reaching people for Christ in every community. So our focus has been, unashamedly, on the local church. There is also a vital place for charities, social businesses, community initiatives and more. We gladly recognise this. However, our focus has been the local church and our quest has been to discover how local churches can truly be a church for the poor in every type of community in our nation.

It is our hope that the second part of the book will have provided our readers with real practical insight and ideas that can help you as you walk a similar journey to ours. This part of the book is aimed specifically at those involved actively in local church life who are concerned about poverty and about the mission of the church. We hope the book has encouraged and stimulated you.

One specific aspiration is also that this book will fall into the hands of those with leadership responsibilities or aspirations in churches. It is they, and they alone, who ultimately have the power to shape and reshape local churches and, specifically, to address its mission to the poor. Many of the leaders we have in mind are already leading churches and some of them have denominational responsibilities as well. However, some leaders are leaders in training, some are church planters, some are evangelists, some are the as yet unrecognised lay leaders who exist in almost every church waiting for the opportunity to enact something of the vision that the Spirit has given them for the mission of the church to the poor. So we say to all leaders, widely defined, this book is for you!

We have sought to move the conversation about the poor forward: to move beyond ideas to plans; to move beyond compassion to action; to move beyond projects to community; to move beyond helping the needy to sharing Christ with them; to move beyond theology to implementation; to move beyond culture to counter-culture.

Hopefully this book has provoked, challenged, stirred and inspired you. We are all on this journey together, so we would love for you to contact us at Jubilee+ if you have any questions, would like to network, or have stories to share with us of how you are building a church for the poor.

We are excited to be alongside you on this journey to build a church for the poor.

REFERENCES

1. See Martin Charlesworth and Natalie Williams, *The Myth of the Undeserving Poor* (Grosvenor House Publishing Limited, 2014), 32-39

2. Millennium Development Goals, *UN Millennium Project*, www.unmillenniumproject.org/goals

3. See Charlesworth and Williams, *Undeserving Poor*, 24-29

4. See Charlesworth and Williams, *Undeserving Poor*, 26-28

5. Poverty can be calculated on the basis of income. Until recently, the level chosen as the threshold was 60 percent of median income in the UK. This is now widely contested. We have chosen to use the benchmark of publicly agreed necessities for life and the lack of them as the basis for our discussion.

6. For a wider discussion on varying methodologies of measuring relative poverty, see both 'How poor is too poor?' by Joanna Mack (http://poverty.ac.uk/definitions-poverty) and government research based on the Indices of Multiple Deprivation (e.g. www.gov.uk/government/statistics/english-indices-of-deprivation-2015)

7. PSE UK, 'The Impoverishment of the UK', *Poverty and Social Exclusion*, 2013, www.poverty.ac.uk/sites/default/files/attachments/

The_Impoverishment_of_the_UK_PSE_UK_first_results_summary_report_March_28.pdf

8. www.poverty.ac.uk/pse-research/explore-data

9. Stewart Lansley and Joanna Mack, *Breadline Britain* (Oneworld, 2015), 262. Note that a separate list for children was drawn up in the same research and is recorded here.

10. 'Falling below minimum standards', *Poverty and Social Exclusion*, www.poverty.ac.uk/pse-research/falling-below-minimum-standards

11. 'Going backwards: 1983–2012', *Poverty and Social Exclusion*, www.poverty.ac.uk/pse-research/going-backwards-1983-2012

12. See, for example, 'Just about managing: Four million more people living on inadequate incomes in modern Britain', *Joseph Rowntree Foundation*, 15 February 2017, www.jrf.org.uk/press/just-about-managing-four-million-more-living-britain and 'UK one of the most unequal countries, says Oxfam', *BBC News*, 13 September 2016, www.bbc.co.uk/news/business-37341095

13. 'Inequality is bad for growth, says OECD', *BBC News*, 21 May 2015, www.bbc.co.uk/news/business-32826643

14. Charlesworth and Williams, *Undeserving Poor*, 32-39

15. 'National Church and Social Action Survey', *Jubilee+*, 1 June 2014, http://jubilee-plus.org/research/6/national-church-and-social-action-survey-2014

16. Charlesworth and Williams, *Undeserving Poor*, 68-69

17. The word 'class' in this context is used in a spiritual or educational sense—with no reference to social class

18. J Wesley Bready, *England before and after Wesley* (Hodder & Stoughton, 1938), 203-204

19. Darren Edwards, *Chav Christianity* (New Generation Publishing, 2013)

20. Geoffrey Evans and Jonathan Mellon, 'Social Class', *British Social Attitudes 33* (NatCen Social Research, 2016), www.bsa.natcen.ac.uk/media/39094/bsa33_social-class_v5.pdf

21. Evans and Mellon, 'Social Class', 14

22. 'Churchgoing in the UK', *Tearfund,* http://news.bbc.co.uk/1/shared/bsp/hi/pdfs/03_04_07_tearfundchurch.pdf, 19

23. 'Men practising Christian worship', *YouGov* (2015), http://cvm.org.uk/downloads/YouGov-CVMreport.pdf

24. Barna Group, 'Perceptions of Jesus, Christians & Evangelism in England', *Talking Jesus* (2015), www.talkingjesus.org/research/upload/Perceptions-of-Jesus-Christians-and-Evangelism-Executive-Summary.pdf

25. Charlie Ball, 'Most people in the UK do not go to university – and maybe never will', *The Guardian,* 4 June 2013, www.theguardian.com/higher-education-network/blog/2013/jun/04/higher-education-participation-data-analysis

26. Ruby K Payne, *A Framework for Understanding Poverty* (AHA! Process, 2005). A summary of Dr Payne's findings is available at: www.wordonthestreets.net/Articles/481670/Hidden_rules_among.aspx. See also Tim Chester, *Unreached* (IVP, 2012)

27. Lord Ashcroft, 'How the United Kingdom voted on Thursday ... and why', *Lord Ashcroft Polls,* 24 June 2016, http://lordashcroftpolls.com/2016/06/how-the-united-kingdom-voted-and-why/ NB C1 (supervisory, clerical and junior managerial, administrative or professional) voters voted leave, but only just (51 percent).

28. 'Ethnicity', *London's Poverty Profile,* www.londonspovertyprofile.org.uk/indicators/groups/ethnicity/

29. Ibid.

30. 'Poverty rate by ethnicity', *Joseph Rowntree Foundation*, 22 March 2017, www.jrf.org.uk/data/poverty-rate-ethnicity

31. 'It's beginning to look a lot like Christmas – but will you still be paying for it in March?', *Nationwide*, 21 November 2016, www.nationwide. co.uk/about/media-centre-and-specialist-areas/media-centre/press-releases/archive/2016/11/21-christmas-spending

32. 'History of cards', *The UK Cards Association*, www.theukcardsassociation. org.uk/history_of_cards/index.asp

33. 'The Money Statistics April 2017', *The Money Charity*, www. themoneycharity.org.uk/money-statistics/

34. Ibid.

35. Andrew Holt, 'Britain is becoming more materialistic as recovery holds, says new report', *Charity Times*, 17 June 2014, www.charitytimes.com/ ct/Britain_becoming_more_materialistic_recovery_holds_new_report. php

36. Richard Foster, *Freedom of Simplicity* (HarperCollins, 1981)

37. Charles Edward White, 'What Wesley Practiced and Preached About Money', *Leadership Journal* (Winter 1987). Available at: www. christianitytoday.com/pastors/1987/winter/87l1027.html

38. John Humphrys, 'British children: Unhappy materialists?', *YouGov*, 15 September 2011, https://yougov.co.uk/news/2011/09/15/british-children-unhappy-materialists/ The full report can be read at: https:// www.ipsos-mori.com/DownloadPublication/1441_sri-unicef-role-of-inequality-and-materialism-june-2011.pdf

39. Jason S. Carroll et. al., 'Materialism and Marriage: Couple Profiles of Congruent and Incongruent Spouses', *Journal Of Couple & Relationship Therapy 10, 4 (2011)*, www.tandfonline.com/doi/abs/10.1080/15332691.2011.613306

40. Richard Alleyne, 'Britain's "me culture" making us depressed', *The Telegraph*, 6 November 2009, www.telegraph.co.uk/news/science/science-news/6514956/Britains-me-culture-making-us-depressed. html

41. Charlesworth and Williams, *Undeserving Poor,* 46-47

42. Charlesworth and Williams, *Undeserving Poor*

43. Alison Little, *Daily Express,* 16 August 2010

44. 'UK poverty: Causes, costs and solutions', *Joseph Rowntree Foundation,* 6 September 2016, www.jrf.org.uk/report/uk-poverty-causes-costs-and-solutions, 14

45. 'What is it like to be "just about managing?"' *BBC News,* 22 November 2016, www.bbc.co.uk/news/uk-politics-38051748

46. Suzanne Moore, 'Instead of being disgusted by poverty, we are disgusted by poor people themselves', *The Guardian,* 16 February 2012, www.theguardian.com/commentisfree/2012/feb/16/suzanne-moore-disgusted-by-poor

47. See *British Red Cross,* www.redcross.org.uk/What-we-do/Refugee-support/Refugee-facts-and-figures and *Full Fact GB,* https://fullfact.org/immigration/eu-migration-and-uk

48. See, for example, Christian Nightlife Initiatives (CNI), www.cninetwork.org

49. Charlesworth and Williams, *Undeserving Poor,* 26-28

50. For example: Anthony Bushfield, 'Archbishop Justin Welby labels Britain's food poverty problem as a "tragedy"', *Premier,* 10 December 2015, www.premier.org.uk/News/UK/Archbishop-Justin-Welby-labels-Britain-s-food-poverty-problem-as-a-tragedy

51. See 'National Church and Social Action Survey', *Jubilee+,* 1 June 2014, http://jubilee-plus.org/research/6/national-church-and-social-action-survey-2014

52. 'Pope Francis wants "poor Church for the poor"', *BBC News,* 16 March 2013, www.bbc.co.uk/news/world-europe-21812545

53. www.svp.org.uk

54. www.focolare.org.uk

55. www.ycwimpact.com

56. www.justice-and-peace.org.uk

57. www.catholicsocialteaching.org.uk

58. www.csan.org.uk

59. See Charlesworth and Williams, *Undeserving Poor,* 26-28

60. 'About CSAN', *CSAN* 22 March 2017, www.csan.org.uk/about-csan/

61. Keith Perry, 'Church attendance has been boosted by immigrants, says study', *The Telegraph,* 3 June 2014, www.telegraph.co.uk/news/religion/10873405/Church-attendance-has-been-boosted-by-immigrants-says-study.html

62. www.church-poverty.org.uk

63. Personal discussions with Church Action on Poverty staff, Autumn 2016

64. 'What is an LEP?' '*Churches Together in England*' www.cte.org.uk/Groups/237712/Home/Resources/Local_Ecumenical_Partnerships/What_is_an/What_is_an.aspx

65. Ministries Council, 'Priority Areas Committee', *The Church of Scotland,* www.churchofscotland.org.uk/serve/ministries_council/priority_areas/about_priority_areas

66. www.freshexpressions.org.uk

67. Claire Dalpra and John Vivian, *Who's There?* (Church Army, 2016) 33http://www.churcharmy.org/Publisher/File.aspx?ID=180861

68. Dalpra and Vivian, *Who's There?,*   58

69. Geoff Knott, *Church for the Poor Survey Report Executive Summary* (November 2016), www.wordonthestreets.net/Publisher/File.aspx?ID=181357

70. www.message.org.uk/history/

71. http://joineden.org

72. https://20schemes.com

73. Mez McConnell and Mike McKinley, *Church in Hard Places* (Crossway, 2016)

74. Soroush's story is more fully told here: www.archbishopofyork.org/pages/ soroush-sadeghzadeh.html and here: www.youtube.com/ watch?v=GfYXpYaDBeE